50% OFF
Online CPCE Prep Course!

By Mometrix University

Dear Customer,

We consider it an honor and a privilege that you chose our CPCE Practice Questions. As a way of showing our appreciation and to help us better serve you, we are offering **50% off our online CPCE Prep Course.** Many CPCE courses cost hundreds of dollars and don't deliver enough value. With our course, you get access to the best CPCE prep material, and **you only pay half price**.

We have structured our online course to perfectly complement your printed practice questions. The CPCE Prep Course contains **46 lessons** that cover all the most important topics, **20+ video reviews** that explain difficult concepts, over **1,000 practice questions** to ensure you feel prepared, and over **450 digital flashcards**, so you can study while you're on the go.

Online CPCE Prep Course

Topics Covered:

- Human Growth and Development
- Fundamentals of Counseling
- Assessment and Testing
- Social and Cultural Diversity
- Counseling and Helping Relationships
- Group Counseling and Group Work
- Career Development
- Professional Counseling Orientation and Ethical Practice
- Research and Program Evaluation

Course Features:

- CPCE Study Guide
  - Get content that complements our best-selling study guide.
- 5 Full-Length Practice Tests
  - With over 1,000 online practice questions, you can test yourself again and again.
- Mobile Friendly
  - If you need to study on the go, the course is easily accessible from your mobile device.
- CPCE Flashcards
  - Our course includes a flashcard mode consisting of over 450 content cards to help you study.

To receive this discount, visit our website at mometrix.com/university/cpce or simply scan this QR code with your smartphone. At the checkout page, enter the discount code: **cpce50off**

If you have any questions or concerns, please don't hesitate to contact us at universityhelp@mometrix.com.

Sincerely,

CPCE
Practice Questions

DEAR FUTURE EXAM SUCCESS STORY

First of all, **THANK YOU** for purchasing Mometrix study materials!

Second, congratulations! You are one of the few determined test-takers who are committed to doing whatever it takes to excel on your exam. **You have come to the right place.** We developed these practice tests with one goal in mind: to deliver you the best possible approximation of the questions you will see on test day.

Standardized testing is one of the biggest obstacles on your road to success, which only increases the importance of doing well in the high-pressure, high-stakes environment of test day. Your results on this test could have a significant impact on your future, and these practice tests will give you the repetitions you need to build your familiarity and confidence with the test content and format to help you achieve your full potential on test day.

Your success is our success

We would love to hear from you! If you would like to share the story of your exam success or if you have any questions or comments in regard to our products, please contact us at **800-673-8175** or **support@mometrix.com**.

Thanks again for your business and we wish you continued success!

Sincerely,
The Mometrix Test Preparation Team

Copyright © 2021 by Mometrix Media LLC. All rights reserved.
Written and edited by the Mometrix Exam Secrets Test Prep Team
Printed in the United States of America

TABLE OF CONTENTS

Practice Test #1

1. The group that is most affected by the "glass ceiling phenomenon" consists of:
   a. women who are in careers most often populated by men.
   b. men in middle management.
   c. blue-collar workers.
   d. stay-at-home mothers.

2. If a client is severely agitated when the counselor tries to complete the psychosocial assessment, which of the following actions is the most appropriate?
   a. Proceed, completing as much as possible
   b. Get all information from the client's spouse
   c. Instruct the client in relaxation exercises
   d. Wait until the client is less agitated

3. Carl Jung's "personal unconscious":
   a. just after birth.
   b. develops in later, more mature years.
   c. occurs in the sensorimotor stage.
   d. forms in the oral stage.

4. All of the following are assumptions of groups EXCEPT that:
   a. the leader is a member of the group.
   b. trust is a must.
   c. much of the growth in groups occurs through observations, modeling, and social learning.
   d. there are often discrepancies among participants' expectations, hopes, and desires.

5. When a conflict arises between the American Counseling Association (ACA) Code of Ethics and a governing authority, which takes precedence?
   a. Ethics always come first, regardless of the circumstances
   b. Ultimately, the law may be adhered to over the Code of Ethics
   c. Neither, the wishes of the client always prevail
   d. There are no standards in place for this issue, it's left up to the individual

6. A female client who was successfully treated for an eating disorder tells other women about her success and recommends her counselor as the expert in treating eating disorders. Her counselor treats eating disorders as part of her practice but would not consider herself an expert. Ethically, she should:
   a. inform the client and anyone she has referred that she is not an expert in treating eating disorders.
   b. post the client's success story on her website.
   c. accept any referrals without any further explanations.
   d. ask her for a testimonial.

1

Copyright © Mometrix Media. You have been licensed one copy of this document for personal use only. Any other reproduction or redistribution is strictly prohibited. All rights reserved.

7. Irvin Yalom identified four stages of a therapy group. The first stage he identified was orientation. The other three include all BUT which of the following?

    a. Conflict
    b. Definition
    c. Cohesion
    d. Termination

8. A client with generalized anxiety disorder expresses feelings of powerlessness. Which of the following interventions is most appropriate to help relieve these feelings?

    a. Reduce the need for the client to make decisions
    b. Provide psychoeducation about generalized anxiety disorder
    c. Include the client in setting goals and decision-making
    d. Stress the positive aspects of the client's life

9. If utilizing sensory stimulation therapy (SST) to improve cognition in a client with dementia, it is important to choose sensory input that is which of the following?

    a. Meaningful to the client
    b. Identified through testing
    c. Easy to demonstrate
    d. Beneficial to multiple clients

10. Which of the following BEST describes a "good" test?

    a. It is reliable
    b. It has norms
    c. It is valid
    d. It is replicable

11. A client believes his favorite actress is in love with him, even though he has never met her. Substance abuse is not a factor, and the client appears to function well in life—holds a job, has social and personal involvements, and does not appear to be disoriented in any other way. What will the counselor suspect?

    a. Psychosis
    b. Schizophrenia
    c. Delusional disorder
    d. Delirium

12. A client with antisocial personality disorder tells the counselor (who is sensitive about her weight) that other staff members are making fun of her appearance and state she is "fat and lazy." Which of the following is the most appropriate response?

    a. Confront staff members
    b. Report this to the department head
    c. Advise the client that he is lying
    d. Advise the client that his comments are inappropriate

Copyright © Mometrix Media. You have been licensed one copy of this document for personal use only. Any other reproduction or redistribution is strictly prohibited. All rights reserved.

13. If a client's family caregivers are interested in taking classes or training to better help them assist the client and cope more effectively with the client's illness, the most appropriate referral is to which of the following?

a. National Alliance on Mental Illness (NAMI)
b. Substance Abuse and Mental Health Services Administration (SAMHSA)
c. American Psychiatric Counselors Association (APNA)
d. National Institute of Mental Health (NIMH)

14. A client who reports being repeatedly possessed by a demon has been diagnosed with dissociative identity disorder. When determining the most effective approach to therapy, the counselor should be aware that the most common environmental factor associated with the development of this disorder is which of the following?

a. Childhood medical procedures
b. Childhood physical and/or sexual abuse
c. Childhood terror (war, violence)
d. Childhood separation from parent/caregiver

15. When assessing a client's orientation, the counselor should be aware that which of the following is the first thing the client is likely to lose track of?

a. Person
b. Place
c. Time
d. Current situation

16. In a decision-making model of career development, factors that could influence decision-making include all of the following EXCEPT:

a. one's vocational maturity.
b. the person's investment(s).
c. someone's personal values.
d. one's style of taking risks.

17. Mannie and Moe were Eastern European Jewish brothers who came to America in the early 1920s and both became naturalized U.S. citizens. Mannie worked in the garment district, enjoyed going to baseball games and eating (kosher) hot dogs, and proudly flew an American flag in front of his house. He also still attended shul (temple) in his new country, celebrated all Jewish holidays, and his wife would light candles every Friday night in observance of the Sabbath. Moe also flew an American flag, went to ball games and ate hot dogs; however, he also altered his last name so it would not sound Jewish, did not attend a synagogue, married a woman who was not Jewish, joined a non-Jewish country club, and worked on Wall Street as a stockbroker. He and his family would put up a Christmas tree and decorations every year. Which combination of terms correctly identifies each brother's process?

a. Mannie's process was acculturation and Moe's process was assimilation
b. Mannie's process was assimilation and Moe's process was acculturation
c. Both Mannie and Moe underwent a process of acculturation in America
d. Both Mannie and Moe underwent the process of assimilation in America

Copyright © Mometrix Media. You have been licensed one copy of this document for personal use only. Any other reproduction or redistribution is strictly prohibited. All rights reserved.

18. Which of the following correctly states the relationship between significance level and type I error?

    a. As the significance level decreases, so does the level of type I error
    b. As the significance level decreases, the level of type I error increases
    c. There is no direct relationship between significance level and type I error
    d. Type I error may increase or decrease as significance level increases

19. One method of calculating intelligence quotient (IQ) in children is:

    a. chronological age/mental age × 100.
    b. chronological age/mental age + 100.
    c. mental age/chronological age + 100.
    d. mental age/chronological age × 100.

20. Which of the following are the greatest risk factors for obstructive sleep apnea/hypopnea?

    a. Obesity and male gender
    b. Obesity and female gender
    c. Obesity and smoking
    d. Obesity and alcohol use

21. A counselor finds herself feeling very angry toward a client whose physical appearance and manner remind her of her abusive father. This is an example of which of the following?

    a. Countertransference
    b. Transference
    c. Displacement
    d. Projection

22. The theorist associated with bonding and attachment is:

    a. Bowlby.
    b. Adler.
    c. Freud.
    d. Piaget.

23. If a client with psychosis divulges that he intends to kill his parents, the counselor must do which of the following?

    a. Have the client arrested
    b. Warn the parents
    c. Increase client oversight
    d. Advise the client not to make threats

24. "Psychometrics" might also be called:

    a. psychiatric interpretation.
    b. psycho-monitoring.
    c. psychological measurement.
    d. a tool of psychoanalysis.

Copyright © Mometrix Media. You have been licensed one copy of this document for personal use only. Any other reproduction or redistribution is strictly prohibited. All rights reserved.

25. What is likely to happen in a group when the leader is authoritarian?
a. Members become dependent on the leader
b. Members become more motivated to achieve goals
c. Members lose focus on goals
d. Members have high morale

26. When beginning a counseling relationship, it is important to:
a. know if the patient is unaware of the counseling plan.
b. give the patient little or no choice in the direction of counseling as it could prove detrimental to the therapeutic process.
c. jointly decide, between patient and counselor, how the counseling process will proceed.
d. answer as few of the patient's questions as possible until the direction of the therapeutic process is naturally revealed during the initial hour.

27. Only one psychoanalyst's developmental theory covers the entire lifespan. Who is he?
a. Sigmund Freud
b. Erik Erikson
c. Jean Piaget
d. Arnold Lazarus

28. What is the "foot-in-the-door" technique used for?
a. Compliance
b. Passivity
c. Aggression
d. Dominance

29. In Stanley Strong's social influence model of counseling, which of the following is NOT one of the characteristics of the counselor that Strong identified as those a client might view as valuable?
a. Expertness
b. Attractiveness
c. Agreeableness
d. Trustworthiness

30. The key to George Kelly's personality theory is the idea of one "fundamental postulate" and eleven ___ that are designed to clarify an individual's personal constructs.
a. corollaries
b. ideas
c. adjunct elements
d. possibilities

Copyright © Mometrix Media. You have been licensed one copy of this document for personal use only. Any other reproduction or redistribution is strictly prohibited. All rights reserved.

31. Raphael's family has just moved to a new neighborhood where he is now culturally in the minority. In his old neighborhood, Raphael's culture was the predominant one. Now Raphael is feeling uncertain about his sense of self. He feels some conflict between depreciation and appreciation of his self. According to the racial/cultural identity development model, Raphael is experiencing:

    a. conformity.
    b. dissonance.
    c. resistance and immersion.
    d. introspection.

32. Why does Carl Rogers use the term "client" instead of "patient"?

    a. To remove the hierarchical element between client and therapist
    b. To differentiate his therapy from psychoanalytic therapy
    c. To promote a more business-like image
    d. To minimize negative stigmas associated with mental illness

33. What does the glass ceiling refer to?

    a. Limitations in the workplace
    b. A developmental milestone theorized by Freud
    c. Adler's theory of passive resistance
    d. A behavioral treatment for phobias

34. According to cognitive behavioral therapy (CBT), which of the following is the type of automatic thought exemplified when a client states, "My mother thinks I'm a failure?"

    a. Personalizing
    b. All-or-nothing
    c. Discounting positives
    d. Mind reading

35. Which of the following is true regarding legal standards of practice in counseling?

    a. Legal practices and ethical practices in counseling are easily separated
    b. Ethical principles and the law each address all behaviors and practices
    c. Privileged communication is a legal right of all counselors in every U.S. state
    d. Sexual contact between counselors and clients is illegal in most, but not all states

36. Which of the following pairs does NOT represent two of John Holland's six personality types?

    a. Realistic and investigative
    b. Artistic and social
    c. Enterprising and conventional
    d. Exploratory and directive

37. Career-oriented, successful ethnic minority women:

    a. face racial but not gender discrimination.
    b. rarely receive support from other women.
    c. tend to have mothers who had low expectations for them.
    d. often display unusually high self-efficacy.

Copyright © Mometrix Media. You have been licensed one copy of this document for personal use only. Any other reproduction or redistribution is strictly prohibited. All rights reserved.

38. As with many other systems, families aim to remain stable and reach equilibrium. This is known as:
- a. egalitarianism.
- b. homeostasis.
- c. equivalency.
- d. predictive stability.

39. A counselor receives a referral from a family physician that attends his church. As a thank you, ethically he should:
- a. pay her for the referral.
- b. send her a thank you letter.
- c. have the physician tell everyone in his church to seek his services if they need mental health counseling.
- d. treat her to lunch on a monthly basis.

40. Which of the following is a general adaptation syndrome (GAS) stage?
- a. Relaxation
- b. Adaptation
- c. Stress
- d. Resistance

41. A counselor uses a combination of deep relaxation and repeated exposure to help a client overcome her fear of spiders. What type of therapy is being used?
- a. Systematic desensitization
- b. Operant conditioning
- c. Classical conditioning
- d. Both A and C

42. According to Erickson, when an individual fails to develop a strong sense of identity, the individual will have troubles with the development of:
- a. autonomy.
- b. initiative.
- c. intimacy.
- d. integrity.

43. Harry Harlow used baby monkeys and several different kinds of "surrogate mothers" to investigate which factors are important in early development and attachment. According to his findings, baby monkeys:
- a. preferred a soft terrycloth "mother" to a wire-mesh "mother" that held a bottle.
- b. preferred a wire-mesh "mother" that held a bottle to a soft terrycloth "mother."
- c. showed no preference.
- d. preferred neither "mother."

7

Copyright © Mometrix Media. You have been licensed one copy of this document for personal use only. Any other reproduction or redistribution is strictly prohibited. All rights reserved.

44. Kathleen is not excessively troubled, but she is quite shy. She is a member of a counseling group with a focus on minimizing aspects of shyness and preventing their occurrence in social situations. According to Caplan, this would be an example of:

    a. a primary group.
    b. a secondary group.
    c. a tertiary group.
    d. None of these

45. Antony is a child who has lately been having tantrums. His pediatrician tells his mother that this is perfectly normal at his age as he is trying to assert his independence. At which of Erikson's developmental stages and resulting virtues would this child most likely be?

    a. Basic trust versus mistrust (positive resolution: hope)
    b. Autonomy vs. shame/doubt (positive resolution: will)
    c. Initiative versus guilt (positive resolution: purpose)
    d. Industry vs. inferiority (positive resolution: competence

46. Freud is to ego, id, and superego as _____ is to parent, adult, and child.

    a. Jung
    b. Adler
    c. Perls
    d. Berne

47. In Frank Parsons' actuarial or trait-factor approach to career counseling, which step listed is NOT a part of the process?

    a. Study the individual
    b. Survey occupations
    c. Give a prognosis
    d. Make a match

48. According to Roe, career choice is influenced by:

    a. genetics.
    b. parent–child interactions.
    c. unconscious motivators.
    d. genetics, parent-child interactions and unconscious motivators.

49. A staff member complains to the counselor that a client with depression is very difficult to arouse in the morning and does not respond to directions to "get up and get dressed." Which of the following is a more appropriate communication?

    a. "Everyone has to get up by 7:00 to be ready for breakfast."
    b. "You can't just lie in bed all day long.
    c. "Why are you still in bed? Didn't you hear the alarm?"
    d. "Here are your undergarments. Please put them on now."

Copyright © Mometrix Media. You have been licensed one copy of this document for personal use only. Any other reproduction or redistribution is strictly prohibited. All rights reserved.

50. Regarding principles of change related to the Johari Window, which pair listed is NOT true?

a. A change in one quadrant effects all other quadrants; denying, covering up, or ignoring behavior all require energy

b. Threat and mutual trust both increase awareness; the smaller the upper left quadrant the poorer the communication

c. Regarding the unknown area, curiosity exists universally; social customs, training, and fears keep some parts unknown

d. In counseling, a goal is to make the lower right quadrant larger; another goal is to make the upper left quadrant smaller

51. If a client has had persistent (greater than 2 years) fluctuating mood disturbances with many periods of hypomania and some periods of depression, which of the following is the most likely diagnosis?

a. Cyclothymic disorder

b. Major depressive episode

c. Bipolar I disorder

d. Bipolar II disorder

52. Stress inoculation is a concept introduced by:

a. John Krumboltz.

b. Joseph Wolpe.

c. Albert Bandura.

d. Donald Meichenbaum.

53. An experiment in which neither the subjects nor the individuals running the study know which subjects are in the control group and which are in the experimental group until after the results are tallied is called a _____ study.

a. single-blind

b. placebo

c. double-blind

d. confounded

54. Which of these is/are NOT considered underlying principles of ethical decision-making?

a. Beneficence and nonmaleficence

b. Justice (fairness), fidelity (faithfulness)

c. Informed consent and confidentiality

d. Autonomy and self-determination

55. Which of the following pairings of a problem with the most successful therapy for that problem is INCORRECT?

a. Childhood behavior problems and existential therapy

b. Specific phobias and systematic desensitization

c. Depression and rational-emotive therapy

d. Panic disorder and behavior therapy

9

Copyright © Mometrix Media. You have been licensed one copy of this document for personal use only. Any other reproduction or redistribution is strictly prohibited. All rights reserved.

56. Popular techniques of what approach are examination of client's memories, "spitting in the client's soup," and "catching oneself"?

    a.   Adlerian
    b.   Psychoanalysis
    c.   Rational-emotive therapy
    d.   Reality therapy

57. When helping the family of a client develop a crisis safety plan, which of the following approaches are appropriate to use as a de-escalation technique?

    a.   Take control of the situation
    b.   Attempt to reason with the client
    c.   Touch the person on the arm or hand to defuse his/her tension
    d.   Quietly describe any action before carrying it out

58. Jacob Moreno is known for all of the following EXCEPT:

    a.   the theater of spontaneity.
    b.   the STEP Program.
    c.   psychodrama.
    d.   group psychotherapy.

59. A counselor meets a group of people that includes the following subgroups or categories: Members of racial, ethnic, and religious minorities; women; single parents; divorcé(s); elderly persons; people with disabilities; gay men; lesbian women; poor people; children; and young adults. Of all these categories, to which does the term cultural pluralism refer?

    a.   Only the members of racial, ethnic, and religious minorities
    b.   Racial, ethnic, and religious minorities and the gays and lesbians
    c.   Racial, ethnic, and religious minorities and people with disabilities
    d.   The term cultural pluralism refers to all of the individuals listed

60. Counselors should be familiar with the distribution of test scores within the normal, bell shaped curve. Which of these correctly describes this distribution?

    a.   68% makes up one standard deviation from the mean, 13.5% makes up two, and 4% makes up three
    b.   13.5% makes up one standard deviation from the mean, 68% makes up two, and 99% makes up three
    c.   95% makes up one standard deviation from the mean, 68% makes up two, and 13.5% makes up three
    d.   99% makes up one standard deviation from the mean, 95% makes up two, and 68% makes up three

61. A Latino family believes that the client (a family member) has *susto*, which has caused the client to lose his soul. The client has become despondent and anxious and is having difficulty sleeping and eating. Which of the following should the counselor initially explore with the client?

    a.   Family discord
    b.   Phobias
    c.   Substance abuse
    d.   Traumatic events

Copyright © Mometrix Media. You have been licensed one copy of this document for personal use only. Any other reproduction or redistribution is strictly prohibited. All rights reserved.

62. When E. G. Williamson expanded the trait-factor approach, he included all EXCEPT which of these steps?

   a. Decision
   b. Synthesis
   c. Counseling
   d. Follow-up

63. Which of the following is FALSE regarding family therapy?

   a. Family therapists believe that people's problems develop in the context of their families
   b. Family members usually are aware of how they influence one another
   c. Each family member is seen as forming part of a larger, interacting system
   d. When one family member changes, each of the others must change as well

64. Justin has not always had problems, but currently needs some help adjusting to changes in college. His therapist sets specific goals right away. She tells him that he does not necessarily need to entirely understand his problems in order to find solutions. She also uses a scale of 1-10 to measure changes. What type of therapy is Justin undergoing?

   a. Solution-focused brief therapy (SFBT)
   b. Rational emotive behavior therapy (REBT)
   c. Person-centered/client-centered therapy
   d. Social constructionist narrative therapy

65. Seasonal affective disorder is most often treated with which of the following?

   a. Cognitive behavioral therapy
   b. Psychotherapy
   c. Exposure and response prevention (ERP)
   d. Sensory stimulation therapy (light)

66. By comparison, which of these is NOT as commonly identified as a cycle or period in the "life cycle of a family"?

   a. Leaving home
   b. Marrying
   c. Children
   d. Divorcing

67. A 52-year-old counselor comes to work inebriated at least twice a week. He would be described as:

   a. an alcoholic.
   b. an impaired professional.
   c. a burn-out.
   d. a workaholic.

Copyright © Mometrix Media. You have been licensed one copy of this document for personal use only. Any other reproduction or redistribution is strictly prohibited. All rights reserved.

68. A client being treated for depression tells the counselor that in addition to behavioral therapy and antidepressant (SSRI), he has started taking St. John's wort as he believes it may help relieve his depression. Which of the following is the most appropriate response?

 a. Tell the client that St. John's wort is a mild antidepressant and may help
 b. Tell the client that St. John's wort has no effect on depression and should be discontinued
 c. Tell the client to discuss the use of St. John's wort with the psychiatrist who prescribed the antidepressant
 d. Warn the client that combining St. John's wort with an antidepressant may cause a life-threatening reaction

69. A client insists that she is through with her previous boyfriend, but during a discussion of her current relationship, inadvertently calls her new boyfriend by her previous boyfriend's name. What might this be referred to as?

 a. A latent moralism
 b. A slip of the tongue
 c. A Freudian slip
 d. A subconscious oversight

70. What type of theory includes "reflection"?

 a. Humanistic
 b. Behavioral
 c. Psychoanalytic
 d. Gestalt

71. When working with blended families, a marriage and family counselor educates family members about the new dynamics within the family structure. More specifically, the counselor discusses:

 a. how adults and children come into the blended family with expectations from their previous families.
 b. how parent–child relationships rarely change.
 c. how a blended family begins after many losses and changes.
 d. both A and C.

72. What does "group process" refer to?

 a. The manner in which the group processes information
 b. Analysis of the group's interactions
 c. The material that is being discussed within the group
 d. Both B and C

73. When assessing a client with obsessive-compulsive disorder (OCD), which of the following behaviors would be classified as an obsession?

 a. Desire for symmetry
 b. Hoarding
 c. Repeating actions
 d. Continuously making lists

Copyright © Mometrix Media. You have been licensed one copy of this document for personal use only. Any other reproduction or redistribution is strictly prohibited. All rights reserved.

74. An Asian client is most likely to choose a counselor who is:
a. black.
b. white.
c. Asian.
d. Hispanic.

75. Telecommuting often involves:
a. flexible schedules.
b. the Internet.
c. computers.
d. all of the above.

76. When differentiating between bipolar disorder and attention-deficit hyperactivity disorder, which of the following characteristics typically applies only to attention-deficit hyperactivity disorder?
a. Onset of symptoms is before age 7
b. Symptoms tend to be cyclical
c. Talkative with pressured speech
d. Distractibility increases

77. Following the death of her spouse after 50 years of marriage, a client has experienced complicated grieving and complains of severe anxiety and a feeling of helplessness and an inability to make decisions. Which of the following interventions may be most effective in helping to resolve these problems?
a. Support group
b. Referral to psychiatrist for antidepressants
c. Role playing decision-making situations
d. Journaling

78. A client with major depressive disorder has difficulty concentrating and appears to be moving and talking in slow motion. Which of the following is the correct term for these behavioral symptoms?
a. Fugue state
b. Psychomotor retardation
c. Cataplexy
d. Anhedonia

79. Gilbert Wrenn's term "cultural encapsulation" refers to all of the following EXCEPT:
a. replacement of reality with model stereotypes.
b. ignoring cultural variations for a universal truth.
c. technique-oriented use of the counseling process.
d. remaining isolated within one cultural context.

80. Developmental changes occur in all but which of the following broad areas?
a. Physical development
b. Cognitive development
c. Psychosocial development
d. Sociocultural development

Copyright © Mometrix Media. You have been licensed one copy of this document for personal use only. Any other reproduction or redistribution is strictly prohibited. All rights reserved.

81. Systematic desensitization and "flooding" are:

   a. behavioral therapies.
   b. psychodynamic therapies.
   c. reality therapies.
   d. Adlerian therapies.

82. The following are all examples of intrusive or reactive measurement EXCEPT:

   a. questionnaires.
   b. records reviews.
   c. interviews.
   d. open observation.

83. A receptionist at a dental office is not allowed to sing or hum at the office, but when she gets home, she turns on the radio and sings her favorite songs as loudly as she can. This is an example of:

   a. the contrast effect.
   b. spillover.
   c. the compensatory effect.
   d. the recency effect.

84. Andrew would like to talk to a counselor about some things he has on his mind. He wonders just what his life means and what the point is to our existence. He feels considerable anxiety over many things, and he frequently feels guilty as well. He is very introspective and is always seeking to understand himself better. Which type of therapy would probably make a good fit for Andrew?

   a. Reality therapy
   b. Behavioral counseling
   c. Existential therapy
   d. Transactional analysis

85. A 45-year-old male is married with two children. He lost his job 6 months ago and has been unable to make house payments, He has become increasingly temperamental with explosive outbursts of anger and attacked his wife during an argument, hitting her in the face and throwing her against the wall. Which type of emotional crisis he is likely experiencing?

   a. Adventitious/Social
   b. Situational/Dispositional
   c. Maturational/Developmental
   d. Psychopathological

86. Which of the following is an example of rumination?

   a. The client has unwanted sexual imagery when encountering an attractive member of the same gender
   b. When attending church, the client has upsetting thoughts that are at odds with religious beliefs
   c. When driving, the client worries about driving off the side of the road and being injured
   d. A client is unable to sleep at night because of constantly worrying about the safety and wellbeing of her children

Copyright © Mometrix Media. You have been licensed one copy of this document for personal use only. Any other reproduction or redistribution is strictly prohibited. All rights reserved.

87. A researcher reports a correlation coefficient of –.43 between the amount of television viewing by children and the number of times these children are on the honor roll at school. This means:

    a. too much television viewing causes students' grades to be low.

    b. there is a moderately negative relationship between how much television a child watches and how often her or his grades are high enough to earn a position on the honor roll.

    c. there is very little relationship between how much television a child watches and how often her or his grades are high enough to earn a position on the honor roll.

    d. the more television a child watches, the more often the child's grades are high enough to earn a position on the honor roll.

88. Eric's counselor uses narrative therapy. Eric has written a "story" to describe his life as his counselor asked him to do. Now the therapist helps Eric to find exceptions and strengths to describe a new story that fits better with how Eric would like his life to be. This therapeutic technique is an example of:

    a. clarification.

    b. deconstruction.

    c. re-authoring.

    d. documentation.

89. What is "leisure time"?

    a. Time away from work

    b. A term coined by Carl Jung

    c. A time-management tool

    d. A critical factor in Alfred Adler's developmental theory

90. Dr. Stanwyck has determined that not only was there a statistically significant difference in the scores of his two groups of students following two different courses of counseling, but also that these scores had a statistically significant interaction with each other. Now he wants to see if, in addition to tested levels of self-efficacy, his subjects' levels of optimism have changed following the two kinds of counseling. Accordingly, he gives both groups a questionnaire to assess their level of optimism. (Dr. Stanwyck had planned ahead and had given both groups a pre-test assessing their baseline optimism levels before the counseling courses began.) To make his analysis of the students' levels of both self-efficacy and optimism following the counseling, what kind of test will he need to use?

    a. ANOVA (one-way)

    b. ANOVA (factorial)

    c. MANOVA

    d. ANCOVA

91. One of the major criticisms of projective tests is that they:

    a. have too many questions.

    b. are too subjective.

    c. are too structured.

    d. take too much time to administer.

Copyright © Mometrix Media. You have been licensed one copy of this document for personal use only. Any other reproduction or redistribution is strictly prohibited. All rights reserved.

92. A counselor is working with a client that voices complaints about significant chronic back and shoulder pain, which is the basis of a disability claim. During the time interacting with the client the counselor notes that he is able to bend down to move and pick things up, and is able to reach over his head into an upper cabinet—all without apparent difficulty or complaints of pain. The most appropriate determination would be:

   a. illness anxiety disorder.
   b. malingering.
   c. factitious disorder.
   d. somatic symptom disorder.

93. A client presents with his wife both complaining that the patient has had a change in cognitive function including language and memory. The client denies loss of pleasure in normal activities and denies feeling sad. The client is able to manage his medications but requires someone to set up his medication box and set a timer for him. The worker suspects:

   a. neurocognitive disorder.
   b. delirium.
   c. depression.
   d. schizophrenia.

94. Most therapists consider the best size for group therapy to be between:

   a. 2 and 4 members.
   b. 10 and 15 members.
   c. 6 and 8 members.
   d. 3 and 10 members.

95. According the DSM-5 criteria, a client that has previously met the criteria for stimulant use disorder but now has not met the criteria for stimulant use disorder in the past 10 months (except for craving) would be termed to be in _____ remission.

   a. full
   b. partial
   c. early
   d. sustained

96. Which is NOT one of the types of Analysis of variance (ANOVA)?

   a. One-way
   b. Factorial
   c. Multivariate
   d. Covariate

97. If a client with severe postpartum depression admits she hates her infant but states, 'I would never hurt it," the first priority should be to do which of the following?

   a. Encourage the client to ask for help with childcare
   b. Advise the client's husband to monitor childcare
   c. Remove the infant from the client's care
   d. Advise the client to find a family member to care for the child

16

Copyright © Mometrix Media. You have been licensed one copy of this document for personal use only. Any other reproduction or redistribution is strictly prohibited. All rights reserved.

98. One of the main premises of _____ theory is that individuals choose occupations that will permit them to use their competencies.

    a. Caplow's
    b. Super's
    c. Roe's
    d. Hoppock's

99. A new counselor finds that she continually receives answers of "yes" or "no" from her clients. Which of the following is LEAST likely to get her client talking?

    a. Ask more open-ended questions
    b. Make use of silence
    c. Adopt a Rogerian-like technique
    d. Ask "why" to clarify a "yes" or "no" response

100. Satir is most responsible for the development of:

    a. strategic family therapy.
    b. conjoint family therapy.
    c. psychoanalytic family therapy.
    d. feminist family therapy.

101. What does B.F. Skinner's "Skinner box" measure?

    a. Psychosocial adjustment
    b. Contingencies of reinforcement
    c. Interpersonal adjustment
    d. Animal magnetism

102. Which is NOT true of assigning diagnostic codes to clients solely for the purpose of insurance reimbursement?

    a. It is a legally mandated practice
    b. It may constitute insurance fraud
    c. It is unethical
    d. It is illegal

103. If utilizing the LEARN Model for cross-cultural client care, the N stands for which of the following?

    a. Negotiate
    b. Negatives
    c. Norms
    d. Neurological

104. A counselor's uncle asks him to counsel his daughter who is suffering from depression. This is:

    a. ethical.
    b. not an ethical issue at all.
    c. fine, as long as the counselor lets his uncle know what is going on in treatment.
    d. considered a dual relationship and is considered unethical.

Copyright © Mometrix Media. You have been licensed one copy of this document for personal use only. Any other reproduction or redistribution is strictly prohibited. All rights reserved.

105. A client experiencing auditory hallucinations tells that counselor that he hears voices warning him of danger: "Don't you hear them?" Which of the following is the best response?

    a. "There are no voices. You are hallucinating."
    b. "I know the voices seem real to you, but I don't hear them."
    c. "I can't make them out. What are they saying?"
    d. "Try to stay focused on what's real. There are no voices."

106. What is true of an EAP?

    a. It is an educational assistance program
    b. It is designed to help college students
    c. It may be inside or outside a company
    d. It does not have licensed counselors

107. All of the following are assumptions of John Holland's theory of career choice EXCEPT:

    a. individuals can be categorized into six different personality types.
    b. people search for work environments in which their personality types can be expressed without much interference.
    c. environment has very little to do with career choice.
    d. the behavior of an individual is determined by the interaction between the environment and the person's unique personality characteristics.

108. A man comes to a counselor complaining of sexual dysfunction. The counselor has very little experience in treating sexual dysfunctions. According to the ethical code, the counselor should:

    a. do extra study on the topic as he continues to work with this man.
    b. refer him to someone who has experience and training in the area of sexual dysfunctions.
    c. tell him to use some herbal supplement to improve his condition.
    d. ignore this problem and treat the man for depression.

109. Which of the following pairs correctly describes forms of reliability?

    a. Equivalence and internal consistency
    b. Stability and concurrent
    c. Internal consistency and construct
    d. Concurrent and construct

110. Greg seems to make light of everything that goes on in the group. If someone is late, for example, he makes a humorous remark about calling for a search party. Greg would be described as the _____ of the group.

    a. joker
    b. dominator
    c. placater
    d. scapegoat

111. In experimental research, the researcher states a null hypothesis. A null hypothesis states that:

    a. there will be differences found between the experimental and control groups.
    b. the differences between the experimental and control groups are due to chance.
    c. there will be no differences between the experimental and control groups.
    d. Both B and C.

Copyright © Mometrix Media. You have been licensed one copy of this document for personal use only. Any other reproduction or redistribution is strictly prohibited. All rights reserved.

112. When a client's physical symptoms have a psychological cause it is referred to as:
  a. conversion disorder.
  b. hypochondria.
  c. somatic schizophrenia.
  d. illness anxiety disorder.

113. What is reciprocity?
  a. A process whereby the counselor and client take turns at speaking during counseling
  b. A process whereby each member of a therapy group takes an equal turn at speaking
  c. A process whereby one agency accepts another's credentials as equivalent to its own
  d. A process whereby one state board grants licensure to a counselor from another state

114. A group cognitive behavioral therapy (CBT) approach that focuses on relapse prevention for substance use disorders will likely include which of the following?
  a. Stressing the importance of attending Alcoholics or Narcotics Anonymous® (AA) meetings
  b. Stressing mindfulness and accepting oneself
  c. Helping clients identify situations that make them vulnerable to relapse
  d. Advising clients to serve as mentors for each other

115. What is a good strategy for helping an elderly client overcome feelings of low self-esteem related to chronic illness and loss of autonomy?
  a. Praise the client constantly for any activities
  b. Tell the client she has no reason to feel so depressed
  c. Provide opportunities for the client to make decisions
  d. Encourage the client to focus on positive factors

116. A parent brings her eight-year-old son to a counselor, complaining that his teachers feel he is impaired. What testing would likely be suggested?
  a. WPPSI
  b. Rorschach
  c. WAIS-IV
  d. WISC-V

117. If utilizing dialectical behavioral therapy (DBT) to work with a small group of clients with borderline personality disorder, during the weekly group therapy session, one of the primary focuses should be on which of the following?
  a. Prioritizing a list of problems
  b. Identifying quality of life issues
  c. Enhancing self-image
  d. Improving interpersonal effectiveness

118. The main purpose of sensate focus exercises is to:
  a. have the couple focus on communication patterns.
  b. eliminate performance anxiety related to sexual functioning.
  c. teach deep breathing and relaxation.
  d. allow the couple to experiment with sexual positions.

Copyright © Mometrix Media. You have been licensed one copy of this document for personal use only. Any other reproduction or redistribution is strictly prohibited. All rights reserved.

119. The counselor teaches a client with anxiety how to do relaxation exercises in order to relieve the anxiety. This is an example of which of the following techniques?

a. Reframing
b. Operant conditioning
c. Substitution therapy
d. Reciprocal inhibition

120. Which researcher is known for his work with rhesus monkeys?

a. Harry Harlow
b. Sigmund Freud
c. Jean Piaget
d. Albert Bandura

121. Henry, a 72-year-old widower, reminisces with his daughter about his life. He talks about his successes and regrets. This is an example of Erikson's:

a. intimacy stage.
b. generativity stage.
c. industry stage.
d. ego integrity stage.

122. A common weakness in group therapy is:

a. not setting firm goals for the group.
b. having male and female co-leaders.
c. not noting problems in potential group members.
d. having multiple opinions and perspectives.

123. A client's communication focuses on sounds, such as rhyme: "I want to tell, oh well, life is hell." Which of the following is the correct term for this thought pattern?

a. Derailment
b. Broadcasting
c. Clanging
d. Loose association

124. A client is taking diazepam (Valium). What type of medication is this?

a. Antischizophrenic
b. Antipsychotic
c. Antidepressant
d. Antianxiety

125. What element below does vocational psychology NOT focus on?

a. Personality traits
b. Job satisfaction
c. Psychotic symptoms
d. Development over the lifespan

Copyright © Mometrix Media. You have been licensed one copy of this document for personal use only. Any other reproduction or redistribution is strictly prohibited. All rights reserved.

Mometrix

126. When working with a client with conduct disorder, limit setting includes (1) informing client of limits, (2) explaining the consequences of noncompliance, and (3) which of the following?

    a. Providing feedback
    b. Stating reasons
    c. Establishing time limits
    d. Stating expected behaviors

127. Erik Erikson believed that the "unconscious" was among which theorist's greatest accomplishments?

    a. Sigmund Freud
    b. Alfred Adler
    c. Gordon Allport
    d. George Kelly

128. In Ellis' rational-emotive behavior therapy (REBT), what do the D and E stand for in his A-B-C-D-E modalities' classification?

    a. Decision, externals
    b. Doubt, engaging
    c. Disputing, effect
    d. Denial, excitement

129. Which of the following tests are most likely to be used in career counseling?

    a. Iowa Tests of Basic Skills
    b. Myers-Briggs Type Indicator
    c. Minnesota Importance Questionnaire
    d. All of the above are often used in career counseling

130. Which of these is correct regarding ethical issues in group counseling?

    a. Maintaining confidentiality is an ethical obligation, and confidentiality must be assured
    b. Informed consent should be obtained from prospective group members before starting
    c. Group members will naturally form social relationships during the course of counseling
    d. With multicultural groups, it is the members' responsibility to respect different cultures

131. Which of the following resources would probably provide the LEAST reliable information about sources and trends in testing and assessment?

    a. Internet blogs
    b. Journal articles
    c. Test manuals
    d. Test critiques

132. A client jokingly talks about killing himself during a counseling session. The counselor should assess:

    a. whether the client has a plan of suicide.
    b. whether the client has the means to complete suicide.
    c. whether the client has a morbid sense of humor.
    d. Both A and B.

Copyright © Mometrix Media. You have been licensed one copy of this document for personal use only. Any other reproduction or redistribution is strictly prohibited. All rights reserved.

133. Which of these correctly states the relationship between significance level and type II error?

a. As the significance level decreases, so does the level of type II error
b. As the significance level decreases, the level of type II error increases
c. There is no direct relationship between significance level and type II error
d. Type II error may increase or decrease as significance level increases

134. A counselor who has not finished his dissertation has business cards that say "Dr. Dennis Browning, Professional Counselor." He is:

a. acting professionally and ethically.
b. advertising himself appropriately, since he gives himself the title of Professional Counselor.
c. acting unethically by misrepresenting himself as having a doctoral degree when in fact he does not.
d. not really acting unethically, since he does say he is a professional counselor.

135. John Crites' comprehensive model of career counseling includes three diagnoses of a career problem. Which of the following is NOT one of them?

a. Differential diagnosis
b. Maturational diagnosis
c. Dynamic diagnosis
d. Decisional diagnosis

136. All of the following are goals of Whitaker's symbolic family therapy EXCEPT:

a. boundary setting.
b. developing family nationalism.
c. educating to promote change.
d. separating and rejoining.

137. What is the difference between classical conditioning and operant conditioning?

a. There is no real difference; they are simply different names for the same essential process
b. Classical conditioning involves a stimulus while operant conditioning involves a response
c. Classical conditioning is concrete operational while operant conditioning is formal operational
d. Classical conditioning evokes involuntary responses; operant evokes voluntary responses

138. A client is struggling with a weight problem. She loves sweets, but she hates what they do to her body. The client's conflict is one of:

a. avoidance/avoidance.
b. approach/avoidance.
c. frustration.
d. approach/approach.

139. The counselor notes that a client admitted for anxiety almost constantly drums fingers on the table and taps a foot. Which of the following is the term to describe this behavior?

a. Automatisms
b. Psychomotor retardation
c. Waxy flexibility
d. Nervous tics

Copyright © Mometrix Media. You have been licensed one copy of this document for personal use only. Any other reproduction or redistribution is strictly prohibited. All rights reserved.

140. A client reports increasing anxiety and has identified a number of stressors in his life. According to the Social Readjustment Rating Scale, which of the following is likely to cause the most stress?

- a. Sexual dysfunction
- b. Marital separation
- c. Fired from job
- d. Change in living conditions

141. Which of the following is true of either inductive or deductive research?

- a. Deductive research is practical and begins with the real world
- b. Inductive research originates from previously established theory
- c. Deductive research is descriptive, correlational, and historical
- d. Inductive research often tends to lead to the building of theory

142. A hypothesis is:

- a. a defense mechanism.
- b. a testable prediction.
- c. a conclusion based on data.
- d. none of the above.

143. At the end of a discussion with a client about modifying the client's plan of care, the counselor states: "I understand you to say that you want to try some alternative treatments, such as imagery and relaxation, to help cope with your anxiety." This is an example of which of the following?

- a. Validating
- b. Summarizing
- c. Restating
- d. Assessing

144. If a counselor gives two tests and the correlation between them is 0.80, what is the true variance they have in common?

- a. 40%
- b. 64%
- c. 16%
- d. 80%

145. Which of the following are measures of central tendency?

- a. Standard error of measurement and standard deviation
- b. Median and mode
- c. Range and variance
- d. Stanine and percentile

146. Which group shows suggested minimum sample sizes for the kinds of research named?

- a. 25 for experimental research, 10 for correlational research, and 50 for survey research
- b. 5 for experimental research, 15 for correlational research, and 25 for survey research
- c. 20 for experimental research, 30 for correlational research, and 1000 for survey research
- d. 15 for experimental research, 30 for correlational research, and 100 for survey research

23

Copyright © Mometrix Media. You have been licensed one copy of this document for personal use only. Any other reproduction or redistribution is strictly prohibited. All rights reserved.

147. Which of the following pairs do NOT have something notable in common between their respective theories of counseling?

a. Carl Jung and Rollo May
b. Gordon Allport and Kurt Lewin
c. Sigmund Freud and Aaron Beck
d. Alfred Adler and Joseph Wolpe

148. The counselor is conducting research on clients' level of health literacy based on scores on a questionnaire. The counselor is plotting the scores on a curve to review the distribution. On a normal curve, what percentage of scores would the counselor expect to fall within one standard deviation of the mean?

a. 10%
b. 33%
c. 68%
d. 95%

149. Compared with other counselors, family counselors tend to be more:

a. rigid and inflexible.
b. nondirective and unstructured.
c. interested in maintaining their distance.
d. active, flexible, and structured.

150. The 20th percentile represents:

a. the score at or below which 80% of the scores in the distribution fall.
b. that the examinee correctly answered 80% of the questions on the test.
c. the score at or below which 20% of the scores in the distribution fall.
d. that the examinee correctly answered 20% of the questions on the test.

151. If a client with schizophrenia has shown structural brain abnormalities on cerebral CT and MRI, the counselor should suspect that the client will exhibit primarily which of the following types of symptoms?

a. Impossible to predict
b. Positive symptoms
c. Mixed symptoms
d. Negative symptoms

152. If a client with a history of schizophrenia and substance abuse appears in the office with disheveled appearance, disorganized behavior, thought distortion, and agitation and makes overt threats, the counselor's initial response should be to do which of the following?

a. Immediately leave the office and call security
b. Speak calmly and reassuringly and avoid sudden movement
c. Tell the client that the behavior is inappropriate
d. Ask the client if he is taking his antipsychotic medications

Copyright © Mometrix Media. You have been licensed one copy of this document for personal use only. Any other reproduction or redistribution is strictly prohibited. All rights reserved.

153. Clients with schizophrenia, depression, or bipolar disease are at high risk for which of the following?
   a. Violent behavior
   b. Impaired mobility
   c. Seizure disorders
   d. Dual diagnosis

154. Research that compares findings across many studies is known as:
   a. quasi-experiment.
   b. survey method.
   c. meta-analysis.
   d. comparative research.

155. A client has admitted to having fantasies about pedophilia and enjoying child pornography. The client justifies this interest by stating that children want to engage in sexual activity with adults. Which of the following approaches to cognitive therapy is most indicated?
   a. Cognitive restructuring
   b. Positive conditioning
   c. Aversive therapy
   d. Satiation

156. Cody does what his parents say because he doesn't want to lose his television privileges. This is an example of what level in Kohlberg's theory of moral development?
   a. Integrity versus despair
   b. Preconventional
   c. Conventional
   d. Postconventional

157. Which one of these is a Freudian defense mechanism?
   a. Anxiety
   b. Repression
   c. Superego
   d. Nirvana principle

158. Which of the following is the least supported technique for dealing with resistance in a group?
   a. Confrontation
   b. Modeling
   c. Discussion
   d. Extinction

159. In a "self-fulfilling prophecy":
   a. the false becomes true.
   b. what was true becomes false.
   c. there is no change to the status.
   d. truth and falseness are relative.

Copyright © Mometrix Media. You have been licensed one copy of this document for personal use only. Any other reproduction or redistribution is strictly prohibited. All rights reserved.

160. A client with intellectual disability has moved into an assisted living facility but has had trouble adjusting and making new friends, resulting in increasing isolation and depression. Which of the following techniques is likely to be most effective in working with this client?

a. Imagery and relaxation
b. Psychoanalysis
c. Role playing and modeling
d. Thought stopping

161. The acronym EMDR stands for which of the following?

a. Eye movement desensitization and reprocessing
b. Emotional-mental deconstruction and reconstruction
c. Excessive movement disturbance remediation
d. Executive mental decision-making and restructuring

162. Which theory helps to explain prejudice?

a. Leadership contingency model
b. Rubin scales
c. Catharsis
d. Social identity theory

163. Which test is one of the most researched tests in history?

a. Rorschach
b. MMPI
c. MBTI
d. Wechsler IQ

164. Which of these groups does NOT represent three of Donald Super's nine major life roles?

a. Mentor, employer, advisor
b. Child, student, citizen
c. Spouse, homemaker, parent
d. Worker, leisurite, pensioner

165. Krumboltz's Learning Theory of Career Counseling (LTCC) is based on what early theorist?

a. Freud
b. Bandura
c. Jung
d. Skinner

166. In Murray Bowen's family systems theory of counseling, he identified eight theoretical concepts. Which of these is an accurate representation of one of these concepts?

a. The basic building block of a family's emotional system is a quadrangle
b. Differentiation of self is how individuals distinguish between self and others
c. Nuclear family emotional systems with undifferentiated partners are more stable
d. Society is regressing by not distinguishing between emotional and intellectual decisions

Copyright © Mometrix Media. You have been licensed one copy of this document for personal use only. Any other reproduction or redistribution is strictly prohibited. All rights reserved.

167. In a research study, every element of the population has an equal chance of being sampled. What type of "sampling" is this?

   a. Random sampling
   b. Systematic sampling
   c. Stratified sampling
   d. Equivalent sampling

168. The group leader points out defenses, resistances, and transferences as they occur in which type of group?

   a. Client-centered group
   b. Psychoanalytic group
   c. Encounter group
   d. Transactional analysis group

169. A counselor is starting an eating disorders group. Ethically, she should _____ all possible candidates to make sure they are suitable for the group.

   a. screen
   b. diagnose
   c. allow a sample session for
   d. interview

170. In milieu therapy (AKA therapeutic community), if a person exhibits inappropriate behavior, the correct response is to do which of the following?

   a. Ignore the behavior
   b. Ask the other clients to determine consequences
   c. Help the client examine the effect the behavior has on others
   d. Apply punishment or restrictions for the inappropriate behavior

171. Jacob's father tells Jacob to clean his room. When Jacob asks why, his father responds, "Because I said so." The father's response is most representative of which parenting style?

   a. Uninvolved
   b. Authoritarian
   c. Authoritative
   d. Permissive

172. A family of four comes in to see a counselor. As the session begins, the two children and the mother seem to gang up on the father and try to pull the counselor into it. Most likely this family is:

   a. triangulated.
   b. enmeshed.
   c. out of balance.
   d. adversarial.

Copyright © Mometrix Media. You have been licensed one copy of this document for personal use only. Any other reproduction or redistribution is strictly prohibited. All rights reserved.

173. A 7-year-old child with autism spectrum disorder refuses to eat any foods or drinks other than one specific brand of crackers and apple juice and has begun to develop nutritional deficiencies and weight loss. The child throws a tantrum if the parents attempt to provide other food or drinks. Which of the following is the most likely diagnosis?

    a. Anorexia
    b. Obsessive-compulsive disorder
    c. Avoidant/Restrictive food intake disorder
    d. Conversion disorder

174. What does "validity" in testing refer to?

    a. How sure one can be, before the test is taken, of what the outcome will be
    b. How many samples were used in evaluation of the test
    c. How consistent the test results are
    d. How accurate a test is

175. A counselor decides to study how elementary school students behave in a classroom when adults are present as opposed to when there are no adults present. A few classes volunteer for the study, and the counselor explains to them how this study may help to avoid future behavioral problems in the classroom. Which of the following is the counselor likely to see?

    a. Catharsis
    b. The Hawthorne effect
    c. The observer effect
    d. Both B and C

176. Which of the following is the goal of the harm-reduction based model of recovery from substance abuse?

    a. Remain abstinent
    b. Carry out step-wise decrease in use leading to abstinence
    c. Use substances more responsibly
    d. Engage family/friends in recovery effort

177. Which of these is NOT a measure of central tendency?

    a. Norm
    b. Median
    c. Mean
    d. Mode

178. What are major common features between Nathan Ackerman's psychodynamic theory of family counseling, Carl Whitaker's experiential family counseling, Salvador Minuchin's structural family therapy, and narrative family therapy?

    a. The goal of perceiving the situation differently and the counselor's position of neutrality
    b. The goal of maintaining the system's balance and the counselor's role as teacher/trainer
    c. The goal of making changes in the family and the counselor's interactive role in the family
    d. The goal of using knowledge the family has and the counselor's helping to find solutions

Copyright © Mometrix Media. You have been licensed one copy of this document for personal use only. Any other reproduction or redistribution is strictly prohibited. All rights reserved.

179. Which of the following tools/methods are characteristic of experimental research designs?

a. Survey questionnaires and interviews
b. Control groups and randomization
c. Use of the correlation coefficient
d. Use of numbers to describe groups

180. In order to elicit a conditioned response, the neutral stimulus that will become the conditioned stimulus must _____ the unconditioned stimulus.

a. follow
b. precede
c. occur at the same time as
d. randomly occur sometime near

181. A confounded study is one in which:

a. there is a wide range of scores.
b. there is a random sample.
c. there are undesirable variables as part of the experiment.
d. undesirable variables are eliminated.

182. What is outsourcing?

a. When outside sources are brought within the company to do a job
b. When jobs are contracted outside the company
c. Using outside supervision within a company
d. An Internet-driven management model

183. A client with multiple sclerosis tells the counselor that she is upset that she can no longer continue her employment because her job is too physically demanding and is concerned about how she will support herself. Which of the following responses focuses on problem solving as a response to stress?

a. "What plans do you have for finding a new job?"
b. "You might be eligible for public assistance."
c. "I'm sure there is other work you can do."
d. "I can see how upsetting that is for you."

184. A client arrives for counseling with the presenting complaint of relationship difficulties. She goes on to describe that she has had multiple abortions, and seems to use abortion as a birth control method. The counselor is personally opposed to abortion. How should a counselor's personal beliefs impact the therapeutic relationship?

a. This personal belief system will make it impossible for the counselor to effectively counsel this client, and the counselor should refer her elsewhere
b. One's personal belief system should not have any bearing on the therapeutic relationship
c. One's position on abortion will enhance the therapeutic relationship as it will make the counselor more effective in teaching the client how to properly view abortion
d. One's anti-abortion stance is best ignored and discounted while working with this client

Copyright © Mometrix Media. You have been licensed one copy of this document for personal use only. Any other reproduction or redistribution is strictly prohibited. All rights reserved.

185. What are the coefficient of determination and the coefficient of non-determination?

a. The coefficient of determination is the degree of common variance, and the coefficient of non-determination is the error variance or unique variance

b. The coefficient of determination is the degree of unique, variance and the coefficient of non-determination is the degree of common variance

c. The coefficient of non-determination is the result of squaring the correlation, and the coefficient of determination is the remainder after subtracting the coefficient of non-determination

d. The coefficient of determination is equal to the correlation, and the coefficient of non-determination is equal to the difference between the correlation and 100%

186. What does a frequency distribution do?

a. It shows the distribution of an audio frequency pitch

b. It shows the number of times a particular value occurs

c. It monitors the ongoing results of a research study

d. Both A and B

187. In Donald Super's developmental approach to careers, which vocational developmental task did Super associate with the period of ages 18 to 21?

a. Crystallization

b. Specification

c. Implementation

d. Stabilization

188. An adolescent male client has become obsessed with body building and has been taking anabolic steroids and lifting weights so much that it has resulted in dangerous hypertension and muscle strain. The client states that he has to build muscle because he looks weak and small. Which of the following is the most likely diagnosis?

a. Muscle dysmorphia

b. Obsessive-compulsive disorder

c. Major depressive disorder

d. Schizoaffective disorder

189. Which is the correct chronological order of the five stages of development identified by Sigmund Freud?

a. Oral, anal, phallic, latency, genital

b. Oral, phallic, anal, genital, latency

c. Oral, latency, anal, genital, phallic

d. Oral, anal, genital, latency, phallic

190. Tuckman identifies the five states of a therapy group with all EXCEPT which of the following rhyming words?

a. Forming, storming

b. Conforming, swarming

c. Norming, performing

d. Mourning, adjourning

Copyright © Mometrix Media. You have been licensed one copy of this document for personal use only. Any other reproduction or redistribution is strictly prohibited. All rights reserved.

191. Which of these is NOT a common role for a member of a therapy group?

    a. Facilitative
    b. Autocratic
    c. Maintenance
    d. Blocking

192. A client presents with concerns about his health. He reports chronic intestinal difficulties, but has not sought medical treatment for his concerns. He says for at least the last five years he rarely feels at ease while at his job, and dislikes shopping or traveling (feeling his best when in the home setting). He is resistant to seeing a physician, but the counselor finds no negative ideation related to medical intervention. What might this client be suffering?

    a. General anxiety
    b. Agoraphobia
    c. Acute stress disorder
    d. Post-traumatic stress disorder

193. What is the difference between "undecided" and "indecisive" in terms of career counseling?

    a. There is no difference; they are simply synonyms
    b. An undecided individual needs more information
    c. The indecisive individual needs more information
    d. An undecided person always has trouble deciding

194. A client has been diagnosed with fetishistic disorder and has court-ordered therapy after an arrest for stealing women's undergarments in order to achieve sexual gratification. The client is resistive to changing behavior and reports little interest in establishing a normal sexual relationship but is fearful of further arrests. Which of the following may be the best focus of therapy?

    a. Finding legal access to women's undergarments
    b. Decreasing the response to women's undergarments
    c. Replacing this fetish with a more socially-acceptable one
    d. Referring the client to a psychiatrist for medical treatment

195. If a counselor recognizes a personal bias against a particular ethnic/cultural group, the first step in mitigating the negative effects is for the counselor to do which of the following?

    a. List and try to comprehend the negative effects of the bias
    b. Identify a number of strategies to deal with the bias
    c. Identify the nature of the bias, describe it, and consider the cause
    d. Determine the lessons learned from dealing with the bias

196. If a client experiences a panic attack and thinks, "I can control this. I am just anxious, but the symptoms will go away if I remain calm," this is an example of which technique learned through cognitive behavioral therapy?

    a. Decatastrophizing
    b. Assertiveness
    c. Socratic questioning
    d. Positive reframing

Copyright © Mometrix Media. You have been licensed one copy of this document for personal use only. Any other reproduction or redistribution is strictly prohibited. All rights reserved.

197. Which of the following is sometimes called "third force psychology"?

a. Psychoanalytic
b. Humanistic
c. Behaviorism
d. Cognitive

198. A counselor cheats on her counselor exam, and she feels bad about it. She tells herself it's OK because she will be a great counselor someday and help many people. The counselor's reasoning is an example of:

a. cognitive dissonance.
b. consensual validation.
c. social facilitation.
d. rationalization.

199. Which of the following is NOT an accurate statement about how the standard error of measurement is used?

a. It is useful for the interpretation of individual test scores
b. It can help determine the range where a test score falls
c. Every test that is given has its own unique SEM value
d. It is calculated after the test has been taken and scored

200. A client shares with her counselor her ongoing state of conflict with her brother. The counselor encourages her to act out her thoughts and feelings as if the counselor were actually her brother. What type of therapeutic theory is in use?

a. Classical conditioning
b. Rogerian
c. Gestalt
d. Aversive conditioning

Copyright © Mometrix Media. You have been licensed one copy of this document for personal use only. Any other reproduction or redistribution is strictly prohibited. All rights reserved.

Answer Key and Explanations for Test #1

1. A: The "glass ceiling phenomenon" refers to situations in which individuals are denied career advancement due to discrimination. This discrimination could be by gender, race, or physical infirmity, such as deafness. Stay-at-home mothers are not in the workforce, so they are not affected by this phenomenon, and blue-collar workers do not seek career advancement.

2. D: If a client is severely agitated when the counselor tries to complete the psychosocial assessment, the best solution is to wait until the client is less agitated because a client who is agitated may not be a reliable reporter or may have difficulty focusing on the questions. In some cases, the client may require medication prior to the assessment although some clients may be more relaxed once they feel more secure.

3. A: Carl Jung's idea of the "personal unconscious" is something that forms just after birth, and consists of experience that the individual is not aware of. Some memories are forgotten and others easily recalled. Some memories may be repressed for various reasons, and others may be subliminal (beyond our sensory awareness) in nature. Whatever the reasons, however, the personal unconscious consists of material from one's thoughts and experiences that slip out of consciousness to become unconscious. It's also important to note that Jung believed that awareness of the personal unconscious was necessary for one to further the goal of self-awareness.

4. A: The leader is NOT a member of the group but is a trained expert. It is assumed that in a group counseling setting, trust is at the forefront. Without trust, no growth or exploration would take place. Trust also allows participants to share personal information with other members of the group. Participants each enter the group with their own expectations, desires, needs, and hopes. These diverse expectations help members of the group discover things in themselves that would go unnoticed in other situations. Finally, growth occurs in groups through observations, identification with others, modeling, imitation, and other social skill learning processes.

5. B: Counselors should make every effort to be knowledgeable of, and adhere to the Code of Ethics as set forth by the ACA. The practice of counselors should remain fully within the bounds of that code, but there may be times when ethics come in conflict with law, regulations, or other forms of authority. When this happens, the counselor is responsible for taking steps to alleviate this conflict. If the counselor's conflict between the ACA Code of Ethics and the rule of law cannot be resolved, then the counselor may adhere to legal authority.

6. A: The best course of action is to rectify any misconceptions that her client has about her and her expertise. Along these same lines, anyone she referred to her also needs to be made aware that she is not an expert. Using her client's story on her website and asking her for a testimonial are unethical. Using unsolicited testimonials is not unethical, but it may threaten the standards of practice that the counselor wants associated with her name. Accepting referrals without any explanation puts this counselor in a difficult position, as those who are referred to her may actually believe that she is an expert.

7. B: "Definition" is NOT one of the stages Yalom identified. He named orientation, conflict, cohesion, and termination as the four stages of a therapy group. The first stage, orientation, is when members get to know one another as individuals and acclimate to the group as an entity. The second, conflict, is when group members experience differences of opinion and personalities clash resulting in disagreements, arguments, or other conflicted interactions among members. The third, cohesion, is when the group experiences bonding among the members and gains a sense group

33

Copyright © Mometrix Media. You have been licensed one copy of this document for personal use only. Any other reproduction or redistribution is strictly prohibited. All rights reserved.

identity. The fourth, termination, is when the course of counseling and hence the group itself arrives at an end.

8. C: If a client with generalized anxiety disorder expresses feelings of powerlessness, the intervention that is most appropriate to help relieve these feelings is to include the client in setting goals and decision-making. The counselor may provide choices to the client, such as regarding the schedule of visits or other activities, and should provide positive feedback when the client is able to make decisions. The client may need some guidance in setting goals that are realistic as unrealistic goals may result in failure, making the client feel even more powerless.

9. A: If utilizing sensory stimulation therapy (SST) to improve cognition in a client with dementia, it is important to choose sensory input that is meaningful to the client. For example, the counselor may show the client family pictures and talk with the client about the family, encouraging the client to retrieve memories, or may play music that the client has previously enjoyed. Certain smells, such as perfume or food smells, may also be used to elicit memories.

10. C: A good test is valid and reliable and has a set of norms. Most important among these is validity. Validity refers to a test measuring what it purports to measure. A test can be reliable without being valid, therefore reliability alone does not necessarily indicate quality.

11. C: Delusional disorder involves non-bizarre delusions in the absence of other mood or psychotic symptoms. These delusions are things that really could happen but simply aren't true. In the psychotic individual, delusions are bizarre (could not happen), so it's important to differentiate between the psychotic delusion and one that takes place without that distinction. It's also important to note that what may seem like a person's "unrealistic belief system" may be acceptable given the culture or religious beliefs of the client. The delusion must be evaluated by taking all factors into account. Psychotherapy and medication are often the choices of treatment for those with a delusional disorder.

12. D: If a client with antisocial personality disorder tells the counselor (who is sensitive about her weight) that other staff members are making fun of her appearance and state she is "fat and lazy," the counselor should remain calm, avoid showing a reaction, and advise the client that his comments are inappropriate. Pathological personality traits common to antisocial personality disorder include antagonism characterized by manipulation, deceit, callousness, and hostility. The client often uses dishonesty, lack of feelings, and hostility to manipulate others.

13. A: If a client's family caregivers are interested in taking classes or training to better help them assist the client and cope more effectively with the client's illness, the most appropriate referral is to National Alliance on Mental Illness (NAMI). NAMI's Family-to-Family program is especially intended for family caregivers of those with severe mental illness. Family-to-Family comprises a 12-week course that is free. NAMI Basics is a course intended for parents/caregivers of children and adolescents with mental illness.

14. B: If a client who reports being repeatedly possessed by a demon has been diagnosed with dissociative identity disorder, when determining the most effective approach to therapy, the counselor should be aware that the most common environmental factor associated with the development of this disorder is childhood physical and/or sexual abuse. The client must be guided to deal with painful memories that may be repressed and to find different methods of coping.

15. C: When assessing a client's orientation, the counselor should be aware that the first thing the client is likely to lose track of is time, followed by place and then person. Clients may, for example, forget the day of the week or the month and date. When orientation improves, it usually does so in

Copyright © Mometrix Media. You have been licensed one copy of this document for personal use only. Any other reproduction or redistribution is strictly prohibited. All rights reserved.

the reverse order, so people become oriented to person first, followed by place, and then time. In some cases, orientation may be extended to include the current situation of the client.

16. A: Vocational maturity is a concept associated with John Crites, who developed a comprehensive model of career counseling including three types of diagnoses (differential, dynamic, and decisional). Vocational maturity is not a term associated with decision models of career development. Factors associated with a decision-making model of career choice include the individual's risk-taking style; the individual's investment, such as money, time, or deferment of rewards; the individual's personal values; and the individual's self-efficacy or belief in one's ability to perform the required behavior(s).

17. A: Acculturation is how much an individual from a racial or ethnic minority adopts and incorporates the customs, values, and beliefs of the dominant culture. Assimilation is how much individuals from a minority change to the point that they are absorbed into the dominant culture, losing all traces of their original behaviors and values. Mannie became an American in following many American customs and behaviors, but retained his original minority religion and cultural values. Moe changed all of his behaviors and characteristics by wiping out his original ethnic and religious identity.

18. A: As the level of significance goes down, type I error also goes down. A type I error is wrongly rejecting the null hypothesis. With a lower significance level, the chances of this are lower. Answer B is the reverse of the correct answer. Answer C is not true in that there is definitely a direct relationship between significance level and Type I error. It is not true that the amount of type I error can go either up or down as the significance level decreases.

19. D: Suppose a child is 10 years old exactly and earns a mental age of 10 years exactly; the child's IQ would be 100 because the fraction of 10 over 10 is 1, which multiplied by 100 is 100. If this same 10-year-old earns a mental age of 5, then multiplying the 10 over 5 (2) by 100 would yield an IQ of 200 (not possible). So, reversing the formula, a mental age of 5 for a 10-year-old (MA/CA) would yield an IQ of 50 (more reasonable considering the data provided). So, having a high mental age over any chronological age would yield a high IQ. Conversely, having a low mental age over any chronological age would yield a low IQ.

20. A: The greatest risk factors for obstructive sleep apnea/hypopnea are obesity and male gender although OSA/H also occurs in females. The condition is confirmed by polysomnography. Treatment includes weight loss, exercise, avoiding sleeping flat on the back, smoking cessation, avoiding drinking alcohol before bedtime, and continuous positive airway pressure (CPAP) therapy. Some may benefit from taking decongestants and allergy medications but medications that cause a sedative effect, such as sleeping pills and anxiety medications, may exacerbate symptoms.

21. A: If a counselor finds herself feeling angry toward a client whose physical appearance and manner remind her of her abusive father, this is an example of **countertransference** because the counselor is displacing feelings toward her father onto the client. It's important to recognize countertransference and to examine the cause in order to increase self-awareness. In some cases, the counselor may need to discuss the issue with colleagues. **Transference** occurs when the client displaces feelings for others onto the counselor.

22. A: John Bowlby (1907–1990) focused his theory on bonding and attachment. Adler is associated with birth order and family constellation, while Freud is associated with psychosexual development. Piaget is associated with cognitive development.

Copyright © Mometrix Media. You have been licensed one copy of this document for personal use only. Any other reproduction or redistribution is strictly prohibited. All rights reserved.

23. B: While what a client says is usually protected by the regulations regarding privacy and confidentiality, if a client makes a credible threat, such as intending to kill his parents, then the healthcare provider must warn the parents of the danger under the "duty to warn" laws. These laws may vary somewhat from one state to another with some states permitting healthcare providers to use professional judgment about warning others and other states requiring mandatory reporting.

24. C: Psychology studies the inner workings of the mind and behavior, but psychometrics seeks to measure it. Psychometrics involves the design, administration, and interpretation of psychological testing. The testing could measure intelligence, traits, disorders, or any other number of psychology-related factors. Sir Francis Galton is often credited as the first pioneer in the field of psychometrics, with a free-association experiment he conducted and later wrote about in 1879. Charles Spearman developed that early work into the idea of measuring human intelligence. Alfred Binet later created an intelligence test, and from there the idea was developed and refined further. Today, psychometrics is a popular field of study, and a valuable tool for clinicians.

25. A: Typically, when there is an authoritarian leader, group members become very dependent on the leader. They usually are unmotivated and show greater hostility toward the leader. Their morale is usually low. In a group with a laissez-faire leader, the members continue aimlessly and lack direction. They have problems staying focused on their goals. On the other hand, a democratic leader inspires group participation, commitment, morale, and motivation.

26. C: Both counselor and patient should work together in devising the basic counseling plan. Working together, with an open and honest orientation, promotes a more integrated and positive approach to the therapeutic relationship, and furthers the ultimate chances of a successful counseling outcome. A regular review of the counseling plan, and level of progress, is also necessary to ensure a positive therapy outcome and patient satisfaction. This approach also shows respect for the freedom of choice of the patient, and his/her active role in the direction of the counseling relationship.

27. B: Erik Erikson is responsible for an eight-stage developmental theory. His final stage, "integrity vs. despair," starts at age sixty, and each stage includes a turning point (or crisis) of some sort. It is sometimes argued that other theorists, such as Sigmund Freud, also have developmental theories encompassing the full lifespan. However, Freud's final stage still speaks of childhood, and Erik Erikson's theory has a stated stage that clearly includes the mature adult and the possibility of peak adjustment at that stage, assuming the other stages have been successfully resolved.

28. A: The "foot-in-the-door" technique is attributed to Freedman and Fraser and their 1966 study of compliance. In their study they asked people if they could put a large, unattractive sign about safe driving in their front yard. When simply asked outright, most people said no. However, when people were first asked to sign a safe-driving petition, they were more likely to comply with the sign being placed on their front yard. The smaller request was, in effect, the "foot-in-the-door" for the researchers that later gained them what they really wanted. The idea is that if one begins by making a small request of someone, they are more likely to get him to agree to something big. Without leading up to the large request, it is less likely to secure compliance.

29. C: Strong did NOT state that the client needs to view the counselor as agreeable. The three qualities he named were "expertness" (i.e., the counselor has formal training, specialized knowledge, and counseling experience); "attractiveness" (i.e., the client perceives the counselor to be similar to the client and covets the counselor's approval); and "trustworthiness" (i.e., the client perceives the counselor as caring about and wanting to help the client).

Copyright © Mometrix Media. You have been licensed one copy of this document for personal use only. Any other reproduction or redistribution is strictly prohibited. All rights reserved.

30. A: George Kelly believed that each individual has an underlying "fundamental postulate" that affects everything else. In his theory, eleven corollaries help to define one's personal constructs. The corollaries include the following: "Construction," which basically says we base our expectations on past experiences. "Individuality" says that everyone interprets things differently. "Organization" refers to every person's organization of constructs into a hierarchy. Each person's construct is bipolar, so that's how "Dichotomy" could be described, while "Choice" is as it sounds. "Range," "Experience," Modulation," "Fragmentation," "Commonality," and "Sociality" round out the rest of the eleven.

31. B: Dissonance. The five stages of this theory are: conformity, dissonance, resistance and immersion, introspection, and synergistic articulation and awareness. In conformity, the individual depreciates his or her self and identifies with the majority. In dissonance, the individual's current self-concept is challenged and the person experiences a conflict between appreciating and depreciating the self. In resistance and immersion, the individual embraces minority views and rejects the majority, which results in appreciation of the self. In introspection, the individual moves away from the intense feelings of resistance and immersion and becomes more concerned with appreciating the self. In synergistic articulation and awareness, the individual owns and appreciates elements of both the majority and minority cultures.

32. A: Carl Rogers believed that therapy should involve a warm, close, and positive relationship between client and therapist. He also believed that the therapeutic environment should likewise be a very positive and supportive one. He used the term "client" instead of "patient" because he wanted to eliminate the hierarchical relationship that was more traditional between patient and client, and instead encourage a feeling of equals. The terminology fits well with the overall emphasis on the client directing the therapy and the therapist acting more as a guide in that process.

33. A: The "glass ceiling" refers to career limits that restrict a worker's ability to rise above a certain professional level. The term is usually used in relation to women or minorities, who some believe are oppressed by white males. This is a complex issue and not easily explained. For example, some hypothesize that differences in income level and professional status between white males and those with ethnic and gender differences may be due to other factors (such as leaving the workforce for periods of time to raise children). Some also suggest that the expectation of the existence of the glass ceiling may actually cause workers to withdraw from the workforce. Cause and effect, in relation to the glass ceiling, is still debated.

34. D: According to cognitive behavioral therapy (CBT), the type of automatic thought exemplified when a client states, "My mother thinks I'm a failure," is **mind reading** because the client is assuming to know what is in another person's mind (although this would not hold true if the mother actually stated that the client was a failure). An example of **discounting positives** is, "Of course I passed the test. The teacher made it too easy." **All-or-nothing** leaves no room for another interpretation: "Everyone knows I'm stupid." **Personalizing** brings everything back to the individual, "He's successful because of my advice and help."

35. D: It is against the law for counselors and their clients to have sexual contact in most states of the U.S., but not in all states (which may be surprising to some people). There is a good deal of overlap between legal and ethical practices in counseling, so they are not always easily separated. Many ethical principles are built into the laws governing the counseling profession. There are some behaviors and practices that only the law addresses. Privileged communication is a right granted to counselors—usually through licensure statutes—but only in some states, not in all states.

Copyright © Mometrix Media. You have been licensed one copy of this document for personal use only. Any other reproduction or redistribution is strictly prohibited. All rights reserved.

36. D: Exploratory and directive are NOT included in Holland's personality types. The styles he identified are: 1) Realistic (aggressive; likes explicit tasks; poor interpersonal skills). 2) Investigative (intellectual; likes systematic, creative investigations; poor persuasive and social skills). 3) Artistic (imaginative; likes self-expression; dislikes systematic, ordered activities). 4) Social (likes interpersonal activities; dislikes working with tools or machines). 5) Enterprising (extrovert; likes leadership and persuasive activities; dislikes abstract or cautious work). 6) Conventional (practical; likes structured, orderly activities; dislikes ambiguous or unsystematic work). Each person is said to possess all six types in varying proportions.

37. D: Career-oriented, successful ethnic minority women often display unusually high self-efficacy that allows them to overcome discrimination that can occur towards women and minorities in the work force. If these women had mothers who had low expectations for them or did not receive much support from other women, then these women would not be successful.

38. B: Homeostasis is the state of stability and equilibrium referred to in this situation. None of the other terms are related to family therapy.

39. B: It is unethical to accept payment for referrals or to pay someone who referred clients. If this counselor wants to thank someone for a referral, a thank you note is most appropriate. Offering to buy her lunch on a monthly basis is unethical.

40. D: Hans Selye, a researcher on stress, developed the general adaptation syndrome (GAS) to explain the effects of stress upon the human body. The body first enters into a state of shock in the "alarm stage." Blood pressure drops, decreased temperature, and lost muscle tone are a few of the symptoms of this stage. Stage two is called the "resistance stage," when such things as stress hormones, heart rate, and respiration all increase. If the body is unable to eliminate the stress, the third stage of "exhaustion" begins. In this final stage, the individual may be more susceptible to illness or even collapse.

41. D: Systematic desensitization is a type of classical conditioning. It's a behavioral therapy used to treat anxiety with relaxation and repeated exposure to the anxiety-producing situation. A common example would be a client who has a fear of spiders. The counselor teaches the client relaxation techniques, and systematically brings the client closer and closer to a spider. At each step, the client achieves relaxation before moving on. Eventually, the client is able to be in the presence of a spider without excessive anxiety. Systematic desensitization can be achieved utilizing imagery as well, and is considered an effective therapy, especially for phobias.

42. C: In Erickson's theory of psychosocial development, individuals who fail to achieve the goal of the lower level of development will have problems attaining the developmental task at the next stage of development. In the example above, the individual failed to achieve identity, which occurs during adolescence. Therefore, in young adulthood, the individual will have problems attaining intimacy, which is the developmental task to be achieved at this level. For autonomy, the individual would have to have failed to attain basic trust; for initiative, the individual would have to have failed to attain autonomy; and for integrity, the individual would have to have failed to attain generativity.

43. A: In Harry Harlow's experiments, he found that baby monkeys preferred physical comfort to hunger satisfaction. In other words, the baby monkeys wanted to be close to a soft terrycloth "mother" rather than a wire-mesh "mother," even though the latter presented food. Therefore, attachment involves more than hunger satisfaction. It involves having close contact with a "loving" caregiver.

Copyright © Mometrix Media. You have been licensed one copy of this document for personal use only. Any other reproduction or redistribution is strictly prohibited. All rights reserved.

44. B: In Caplan's model, a secondary group works to reduce the severity and/or duration of a problem which is usually not that severe, and this type of group generally includes some aspects of prevention.

45. B: The stage of autonomy vs. shame and doubt typically occurs between ages 1-1½ and 3 years, and tantrums are manifested as the child tries to assert their independence. This period is often called the "terrible twos." Positive resolution of this conflict results in the child's development of the positive ego quality of "will" (the determination to exercise free choice). Basic trust vs. mistrust is the first stage (birth to 1-1/2 years of age) when an infant develops trust if their needs are met (e.g., being nursed when hungry and changed when needed, etc.). Positive resolution results in developing a sense of hope. Initiative vs. guilt is the third stage from ages 3 to 6 when children learn to meet challenges, take responsibility, and identify others' rights. Positive resolution results in developing a sense of purpose. Industry vs. inferiority (6-11) is the fourth of the eight stages when children master social and school skills or develop a sense of inferiority if they do not. Positive resolution results in developing a sense of competence.

46. D: Parent, adult, and child is a set of terms associated with transactional analysis, associated primarily with Eric Berne (1910–1970). Fritz Perls is associated with rational-emotive behavior therapy. Carl Jung is associated with analytic psychology, and Adler is associated with individual psychology.

47. C: Parsons' method did not include giving a prognosis. The three steps in his approach were: 1) study the individual for specific traits; 2) survey available occupations (factors); and, 3) match the individual with an occupation. Prognosis was, however, part of E. G. Williamson's approach.

48. D: Roe has a psychoanalytic perspective on career choice, so she believes that genetics, parent–child relationships, and unconscious motives interact. According to psychoanalytic theory all of the aforementioned dynamics influence an individual.

49. D: If a staff member complains to the counselor that a client with depression is very difficult to arouse in the morning and does not respond to directions to "get up and get dressed," a more appropriate communication is, "Here are our undergarments. Please put them on now." Clients with depression may have difficulty responding to global task, such as "get up and get dressed," but may respond more readily if the task is broken into smaller steps, such as beginning with undergarments, so that the client only has to focus on one thing at a time.

50. D: Regarding the Johari Window, the goal in counseling is to make the lower right quadrant smaller (not larger) and to make the upper left quadrant larger (not smaller). The upper left quadrant represents what is known to the self and known to others. The lower right quadrant represents what is unknown to the self and unknown to others. The upper right quadrant is what is known to others but not known to the self, and the lower left quadrant is what is known to the self but not known to others. The goal is to make more information known to the self and to others and less unknown to both. The principles of change named in answers A, B, and C are all accurate.

51. A: If a client has had persistent (greater than 2 years) fluctuating mood disturbances with many periods of hypomania and some periods of depression, the most likely diagnosis is cyclothymic disorder. Generally, the client's hypomanic periods are characterized by a lack of inhibition and feelings of euphoria, but the client is able to function, unlike with full mania. The client may become more talkative and need less sleep. Some clients may become hypersexual.

52. D: All four of these men are associated with behavioral counseling in some way, but Donald Meichenbaum developed the behavioral technique called stress inoculation training. The purpose is

Copyright © Mometrix Media. You have been licensed one copy of this document for personal use only. Any other reproduction or redistribution is strictly prohibited. All rights reserved.

to help the client deal with future stress. The three-step process involves having the client monitor the impact of the inner dialogue on behavior when under stress, rehearsing new self-talk, and implementing new self-talk during the stressful situation. Joseph Wolpe developed systematic desensitization, which is a step-by-step process used to address phobias. John Krumboltz is more known in the field of career counseling but has written books on behavior modification. Albert Bandura is usually associated with social learning but more specifically with learning through observation.

53. C: A single-blind study is one in which only one part of the team is unaware of who is receiving the treatment. In a single-blind study, either the researcher is unaware or the participants are unaware, not both. In a double-blind study neither the researcher running the study nor the subjects know who is in the control group. A placebo effect has occurred when a participant reports improvement where the treatment was really nothing more than water or a sugar pill. In a confounded study, variables that are not wanted in the study come into play.

54. C: Informed consent and confidentiality are important ethical issues that must be considered in counseling, but they are not identified as underlying principles. Principles underlying ethical decision-making are identified as beneficence (doing good and preventing harm); nonmaleficence (not doing harm); justice (treating people fairly); fidelity (being faithful to/honoring commitments); and autonomy (respecting others' freedom of choice and self-determination).

55. A: Childhood behavior problems are best handled using behavioral techniques, not finding meaning through existential therapy, which requires a maturity of thought and intellect that children have not yet developed. All of the other pairs are appropriate. When it comes to dealing with specific phobias, the treatment of choice is usually systematic desensitization, which is a behavioral technique. Depression usually involves having a client look at his/her own irrational thoughts that contribute to the depression. A panic disorder is also usually addressed using some sort of behavioral techniques.

56. A: Adlerian counselors utilize examination of clients' memories, catching oneself, and spitting in the client's soup. Free association, analysis of transferences, and dream analysis are popular techniques used by psychoanalysis. Popular techniques used by reality therapy are role modeling, defining limits, and feedback. Counselors who use rational-emotive therapy often use homework assignments, bibliotherapy, and shame attacks.

57. D: Families should be assisted to develop a crisis safety plan that includes recognizing the signs of an impending crisis and using de-escalation techniques to defuse the situation. De-escalation techniques include avoiding touching the client without permission and quietly describing any action before carrying it out so as not to further alarm the client. The family member should remain calm, speak quietly, listen and express concern, avoid arguing and making continuous eye contact, keep environmental stimulation low, allow the person adequate space, and offer suggestions but avoid taking control.

58. B: The STEP Program (Systematic Training for Effective Parenting program) is a psycho-educational model for parents developed by Don Dinkmeyer using Adlerian principles. Jacob Moreno started the Theater of Spontaneity in Vienna in 1921. He developed the concept of psychodrama, which is used to enact conflicts or crises in a theatrical format with a director, actors, and an audience. Moreno was the first person to use the term group psychotherapy in the 1920s. Moreno also founded the American Society of Group Psychotherapy and Psychodrama in 1941.

Copyright © Mometrix Media. You have been licensed one copy of this document for personal use only. Any other reproduction or redistribution is strictly prohibited. All rights reserved.

59. D: Cultural pluralism refers to broad categories of individuals in society with special concerns or needs, and/or who are seeking greater representation in society. They include all of the groups listed in the question.

60. A: In a normal bell-shaped curve, individual scores are distributed in six equal parts, three above the mean and three below it. Within the bell curve, 34% of scores are above the mean and 34% are below it, adding up to 68%, and this proportion is one standard deviation above or below the mean. 13.5% more of the scores fall two standard deviations above or below the mean, equaling 27%, so a total of 95% (68% + 27%) of scores fall within two standard deviations of the mean. Finally, 2% more of the scores fall three standard deviations above the mean and 2% more fall three standard deviations below the mean, equaling 4%, so 99% (68% + 27% + 4%) of scores are within three standard deviations of the mean. (Note: the 99% referred to is actually 99.7% but has been simplified here.) The rule of 68-95-99% is known as the empirical rule. It may help to look at a drawing of a normal bell curve with the percentages labeled to visualize this.

61. D: If a Latino family believes that the client (a family member) has *susto*, which has caused the client to lose his soul and the client has become despondent and anxious and is having difficulty sleeping and eating, the counselor should initially explore a history of traumatic events with the client. *Susto*, which means "fright," is most often associated with some type of trauma and is often described as a form of PTSD.

62. A: Decision is not a step included in E. G. Williamson's trait-factor approach. This would be a part of decision-making models of career counseling. Williamson's approach included six steps: Analysis, synthesis, diagnosis, prognosis, counseling, and follow-up.

63. B: Family therapists look at families as systems, its members as units that interact together and influence each other. Usually members of families are unaware of how they influence one another, and therefore this is a critical focus in family therapy.

64. A: Solution-focused brief therapy (SFBT) emphasizes setting specific goals early in the therapeutic relationship and having a limited number of sessions. In SFBT, understanding the nature of the problem is not considered necessary to the generation of solutions to it. SFBT counselors often use scales to identify changes in the client's affect. The other three (B, C, D) are not necessarily short-term types of counseling. REBT focuses on correcting irrational beliefs and self-verbalizations by reconstructing and replacing them with rational thought. Rogerian or person-centered counseling focuses on empathy, warmth, unconditional acceptance and the relationship between the therapist and client. Narrative therapy is based on social constructionism and focuses on the client's "story," or their subjective perception of reality, which is considered valid and socially constructed. It may be deconstructed and rewritten to help clients view their lives differently.

65. D: Seasonal affective disorder, which affects some patients when light is reduced to 10 hours daily, is most often treated with sensory stimulation therapy in the form of phototherapy in which the patient is exposed to light from light boxes that provide 10,000 lux of light in the mornings for approximately 30 minutes daily, but this duration may vary with the patient. Most patients see a reduction in depression within one to two weeks. Patients typically start therapy in October or November and stop in March or April.

66. D: Divorce is not as commonly identified as the other choices as a period in the life cycle of a family. While theorists point out that there are many variations, the cycles generally identified are: 1) young adults leaving home and accepting responsibility; 2) getting married; 3) having children

Copyright © Mometrix Media. You have been licensed one copy of this document for personal use only. Any other reproduction or redistribution is strictly prohibited. All rights reserved.

(which includes accepting new family members in the case of babies and young children, and increasing the flexibility of boundaries as children reach adolescence and grandparents age); 4) launching children as they grow up and leave the family unit; and, 5) accepting shifts in the roles of generations as family members move into later life.

67. B: An impaired professional is one who is not able to function in an effective or ethical manner due to a personal problem such as alcohol abuse or other neurological problems. One cannot delineate whether this counselor is an alcoholic from this observation. The counselor may be burned out, but the issue is that he is impaired because of his use of alcohol.

68. D: If a client being treated for depression tells the counselor that in addition to behavioral therapy and antidepressant (SSRI), he has started taking St. John's wort as he believes it may help relieve his depression, the most appropriate response is to warn the client that combining St. John's wort (a mild antidepressant) with an antidepressant SSRI may cause a life-threatening reaction (serotonin syndrome). Additionally, St. John's wort may affect the absorption of other drugs as well so it should not be taken without supervision of a physician.

69. C: A Freudian slip has become a popular part of everyday conversation and refers to the idea that what seems to be accidental may actually provide a window into the unconscious, and what one really thinks and feels. Many people believe that a Freudian slip is only an errant verbal comment, but such a slip can be anything, including physical acts that are caused by the unconscious part of the personality. Freud believed that such slips reveal an unconscious thought, belief, or wish that is sometimes held from conscious thought because it would be deemed unacceptable in some way.

70. D: Gestalt theory, developed by Frederick and Laura Perls, lists "reflection" as a defense mechanism. Reflection in Gestalt therapy, put simply, is doing to oneself what one wishes to do to someone else. Sometimes that can be something obvious, such as a man cutting his own arm when he really wants to act out aggressively toward someone else. At other times, the reflection may be less apparent, such as a young woman feeling resentment toward a friend, but turning that toward herself as depressive feelings instead. Reflection can become pathological when it's chronic, but often exists in a healthy personality.

71. D: Blended families are the result of broken relationships. Therefore, when working with blended families, counselors need to address expectations that members of the blended family have about what relationships should be like (based on prior experiences). Counselors also have to assist blended families with the grief associated with losses and help members of the blended family adjust to changes within the family.

72. B: "Group Process" refers to the interaction of the group members and analysis of how that interaction is working in terms of the group's goals. What the group members say to each other verbally, behavioral cues, and other factors are all taken into account in the interpretation of the group therapy sessions. This includes relationship issues, adherence to goals, individual and group progress, and a variety of other factors that made up the group dynamic.

73. A: When assessing a client with obsessive-compulsive disorder (OCD), a desire for symmetry would be classified as an obsession, which is a repetitive thought process rather than an action. Obsessions commonly present with OCD include concerns about contamination, safety, and the need to act in a particular way. Some people may have persistent sexual or aggressive thoughts. Compulsions are irresistible urges to carry out certain actions, such as washing the hands, touching or tapping items, hoarding, making lists, and repeatedly checking the same thing.

Copyright © Mometrix Media. You have been licensed one copy of this document for personal use only. Any other reproduction or redistribution is strictly prohibited. All rights reserved.

74. C: An Asian client is most likely to choose a counselor who is Asian because individuals are likely to form connections with others who are most like themselves. In Social Psychology, the research into issues such as this tends to indicate that similarity leads to attraction. People tend to feel that their feelings and beliefs are validated by relationships with others who are similar to who they are. Studies have been done regarding such factors as communication, demographics, opinions, and value systems to indicate that those who are similar attract. While not always the case, an Asian client would likely be most comfortable with an Asian as a counselor.

75. D: Telecommuting is a recent development in the study of vocational psychology. It is a growing type of work situation that has been brought on by the success of computers and the Internet and the increasing focus on finding a balance between family and work. Telecommuting refers to work that is done in the home setting, rather than at a separate location away from home. There are many advantages for both companies and workers with the telecommuting situation. Some advantages for companies are cost-effectiveness, increased employee retention, and greater productivity. Employees have flexible schedules, more time with family, and are often happier with their jobs.

76. A: When differentiating between bipolar disorder and attention-deficit hyperactivity disorder (symptoms are often similar), a characteristic that typically applies only to attention-deficit hyperactivity disorder is onset of symptoms before age 7 because onset of bipolar disorder is after age 7. Other indications of ADHD include consistency of symptoms (always present), constant mood, and consistency of distractibility. Cognition is not generally affected although distractibility may interfere with attention.

77. C: If, following the death of her spouse after 50 years of marriage, a client has experienced complicated grieving and complains of severe anxiety and a feeling of helplessness and an inability to make decisions, role playing decision-making situations may be helpful as well as discussions about situations the client has been able to handle independently, such as arranging for her husband's funeral, shopping for groceries, and paying bills. The client may also benefit from engaging in a support group and journaling.

78. B: If a client with major depressive disorder has difficulty concentrating and appears to be moving and talking in slow motion, the correct term for these behavioral symptoms is **psychomotor retardation**. **Fugue state** is a dissociative reaction that includes amnesia and physical flight from environment. **Cataplexy** is a sudden loss of muscle tone and inability to voluntarily move muscles. **Anhedonia** is a loss of interest and pleasure in life's activities that used to give pleasure.

79. D: Wrenn's term cultural encapsulation does not refer to staying isolated within one cultural context. It does refer to substituting model stereotypes for actual reality. It also refers to overlooking cultural variations in favor of believing in a universal idea of the truth, and it additionally refers to a technique-oriented approach to counseling. For example, a psychoanalyst might use only psychoanalytic techniques regardless of who the client was or what the client's problems were.

80. D: The three broad areas of change identified by developmentalists are physical, cognitive, and psychosocial development. Sociocultural is not named as one of the areas of developmental change.

81. A: Behavioral techniques include operant and classical conditioning, systematic desensitization, implosion, flooding, time-out, stress inoculation, and thought stopping. Techniques of the psychodynamic approach include free association, dream analysis, and interpretation of

Copyright © Mometrix Media. You have been licensed one copy of this document for personal use only. Any other reproduction or redistribution is strictly prohibited. All rights reserved.

transferences. Adlerian therapy techniques include emphasizing client's strengths, examination of client's memories, focus on interpretation, and "spitting in the client's soup." Reality therapy techniques include role playing, role modeling, defining limits, and helping the client make a plan.

82. B: Reviewing records is an example of unobtrusive or nonreactive measurement (i.e., data collection occurs without the individual being aware of it). Intrusive or reactive measurement means that the individual is aware of the data collection. Examples include giving questionnaires, interviewing subjects, and openly observing subjects.

83. C: The compensatory effect is a reaction to being restricted from doing something. In this example, the woman isn't allowed to hum or sing at the office, but when she is away from work, she hums and sings to her heart's content. The contrast effect involves two individuals being interviewed for the same position. One qualified candidate is viewed in a less favorable light after a very well qualified candidate is interviewed first. Spillover occurs when an individual engages in activities at home that are similar to those involved in his job. The recency effect takes place when a supervisor judges an employee's performance on the employee's most recent performance, with no consideration for performance at other times.

84. C: Existentialism addresses the search for meaning which would be the best choice of these for Andrew. It would be a natural fit with his personality, since he already wonders and worries about the meaning of life and his role in it. Anxiety and guilt are also important concepts in existential therapy. Since Andrew often has these emotions, this form of counseling would help him to address his feelings and help explain why he has them. Andrew wants to understand himself better, and self-actualization is also a goal of existential counseling. Reality therapy would not be a good fit for Andrew as it is theoretically simplistic, whereas Andrew is very introspective and seeks understanding. Reality therapy ignores the client's personal history and is solution-focused. Andrew seems more interested in understanding himself than in finding immediate solutions. Behavioral therapy ignores inner states, which would dissatisfy Andrew as he is so introspective. Behaviorism deals only with behaviors not the whole person, so this approach would fall short of meeting Andrew's needs. Transactional analysis would be too simplified for Andrew with its cognitive orientation and treatment contracts—and, like reality therapy, it is very goal-directed. Andrew is more inclined to explore questions of existence and to analyze his own psyche.

85. B: Situational/Dispositional crises result from response to an external stressor, such as the loss of a job, leaving the person feeling helpless and unable to cope. **Adventitious/Social** crises result from natural disasters, violent crimes, acts of terrorism, or socially disruptive acts, such as rioting, over which a person has little control. **Maturational/Developmental** crises occur during major life transitions, such as getting married, leaving home, or having a child. **Psychopathological** crises result from a preexisting psychiatric disorder, such as schizophrenia.

86. D: An example of rumination is if a client is unable to sleep at night because of constantly worrying about the safety and wellbeing of her children. Ruminations involve going over and over the same thoughts or concerns for extended periods of time, to the point that the ruminations may interfere with activities and responsibilities. Intrusive thoughts, such as unwanted sexual imagery when encountering an attractive member of the same gender, are generally triggered by a specific event or situation but can be repressed.

87. B: When a correlation coefficient is presented, there cannot be an inference that one behavior or action predicts or causes the other behavior or action. There is no cause and effect when a correlation coefficient is presented. Correlation coefficients range between –1.0 and +1.0. The closer the coefficient is to 1, the stronger the relationship. If the coefficient is negative, this suggests

Copyright © Mometrix Media. You have been licensed one copy of this document for personal use only. Any other reproduction or redistribution is strictly prohibited. All rights reserved.

that as one behavior increases, the other behavior will decrease. In the example above, the more television a child watched, the lower a child's grades were. A strong relationship is usually ±0.55 or above, while a moderate relationship is usually in the ±0.54 to ±0.30 range. No relationship is indicated by a correlation coefficient of 0.0.

88. C: This therapeutic technique is referred to as "re-authoring," and it is used in narrative therapy to helping a client rewrite their story to make it more appropriate. Clarifications are observations made by the therapist to help discover and construct the client's story. Deconstruction is externalizing and focusing on the problem rather than on the person (i.e., the person is not the problem, the problem is the problem) to help to deconstruct it. Documentation of the evidence is often done in narrative therapy by the therapist writing letters to the client. Done between sessions, these are found to be powerful supports to the therapy sessions.

89. A: Past generations worked long hours, focusing on wages and the need to support a family. However, in recent years, the focus on leisure time has increased. Some studies indicate that the absence of leisure time can lead to negative symptoms, and that reasonable amounts of leisure time are important for positive adjustment. Some theorists also believe that leisure time can actually enhance work performance. Overall, the acceptance of leisure time, as a critical consideration in the choice of a career, has increased in recent years.

90. C: A multivariate analysis of variance (MANOVA) is needed when there is more than one dependent variable as in this case. An analysis of variance cannot be used when the experiment has two or more dependent variables. This researcher would not use an analysis of covariance unless he controlled how one or more independent variables affected the dependent variable(s).

91. B: Projective tests usually do not involve any "questions" because the test takers come up with their own answers based on the stimuli presented. Projective tests by their very nature are not structured at all. Usually the instructions the examiner gives are minimal, e.g., "What might this be?" for the Rorschach. Projective tests do take a great deal of time, but this is not the major criticism. Projective tests are very subjective, and the scoring is also very subjective, despite there being scoring manuals for these tests.

92. B: Malingering involves feigning symptoms primarily to derive an external reward (lawsuit settlement, disability benefits, etc.). Illness anxiety disorder involves a misapprehension or misinterpretation of bodily symptoms. Factitious disorder involves a feigning of symptoms primarily in order to receive the attention offered when one assumes a sick role, even in the absence of external reward. Somatic symptom disorder is characterized by complaints regarding several organ systems involving different body sites and functions rather than a single body organ or situation.

93. A: The client is exhibiting symptoms of a neurocognitive disorder. He is having cognitive changes without depressive symptoms. His cognitive symptoms have mildly diminished his activities of daily living, but he is able to complete them with modifications, indicating a mild neurocognitive disorder.

94. C: Most groups seem to function best with six to eight members. However, for groups involving children or adolescents, a slightly smaller group may be advantageous. Likewise, with online group therapy, group size is often thought to be best if kept smaller. In cases of groups that are long-running, there will sometimes be a larger number of members participating in the group, but smaller tends to be the better choice. Keeping groups small allows for more interaction between

Copyright © Mometrix Media. You have been licensed one copy of this document for personal use only. Any other reproduction or redistribution is strictly prohibited. All rights reserved.

members, increased time for each individual to be heard, and enhanced opportunity for the group leader to manage the group.

95. C: Early remission is indicated when no stimulant use criteria have been met (except for craving) for at least 3 but less than 12 months. Sustained remission is no stimulant use criteria have been met (except for cravings) for 12 months or longer. The terms full and partial are no longer used to describe remission.

96. D: Covariate refers to analysis of covariance (ANCOVA) not ANOVA. In an ANCOVA, the influence on the dependent variable of one or more independent variables is controlled. A one-way ANOVA is used when there is only one variable at three or more levels (for example, if there were three or more experimental groups — because there are more than two, a t-test will not work.) A factorial ANOVA is used to determine at the same time whether mean scores on two or more variables have a significant difference, and also whether these variables have a significant interaction with one another. If there was one dependent variable and two independent variables, a factorial ANOVA would be used to measure those factors. If there were more than one dependent variable, the factorial ANOVA cannot be used. Instead a multivariate analysis of variance (MANOVA) would be used. Multivariate means there is both more than one independent variable AND more than one dependent variable. Finally, covariate means that the evaluator is controlling one or more of those independent variables.

97. C: If a client with severe postpartum depression admits she hates her infant but states, "I would never hurt it," the first priority should be to remove the infant from the client's care because the client has admitted hating the child and has depersonalized the child by referring to the child as "it." Additionally, a client with severe postpartum depression is at risk for postpartum psychosis, which may further increase risk to the infant.

98. B: Super's theory ascribes to the notion that one's self-concept is ultimately important in career choices. He believed that people choose a career based on their competencies—what they are good at. Roe's theory is developmentally focused, so her theory does not discuss personal competencies. Caplow's theory ascribes to birth order and genetics as strongly influencing career choices. Hoppock's theory defines career choice as being influenced by one's needs.

99. D: Novice counselors sometimes experience difficulty in facilitating conversation with their clients. This problem is often due to an excess of pointed questions that do not allow for the client to expand upon the inquiry. Open-ended questions are far more productive and urge the client to expound upon the subject matter raised. Restatement of the client's comments (as in a Rogerian approach) can also stimulate further discussion on the part of the client, as can silence, which often has an unspoken expectation of the client's response. Asking "why" questions is discouraged, as they can come across as judgmental and further the gap between client and counselor. Time and experience usually alleviate this problem with novice counselors as they become more comfortable with the counseling situation and their professional skills.

100. B: Satir's most significant contribution to family systems therapy is known as conjoint family therapy. Strategic family therapy is generally associated with Haley and Madanes. Psychoanalytic family therapy is associated with Nathan Ackerman. Feminist family therapy is associated with Sandra Bem.

101. B: B.F. Skinner called his "Skinner box" an operant conditioning apparatus. There are various versions of the box, but one type consists of a small box that is soundproof with a lighted disk or bar at one end that releases food when manipulated by the subject. Skinner used his Skinner boxes with

Copyright © Mometrix Media. You have been licensed one copy of this document for personal use only. Any other reproduction or redistribution is strictly prohibited. All rights reserved.

different animals, including pigeons and rats. Sometimes the disk or bar would be positioned differently, or have various colors, depending upon the needs of the experiment. The disk might also be electrified, for studying negative reinforcement. The purpose of the Skinner box was to study the "contingencies of reinforcement" that B.F. Skinner believed control behavior, which include the interrelationships between stimuli, response, and the consequences of those responses.

102. A: Assigning diagnostic codes solely for the purpose of insurance reimbursement is NOT required by law. This practice may constitute insurance fraud. It is also unethical and moreover it is illegal.

103. A: Negotiate: LEARN Model for cross-cultural client care:

104. D: Just as medical doctors are encouraged not to treat family members or friends, so too counselors and mental health professional are discouraged from treating family members or friends. Because the counselor would be treating his cousin, this would be considered a dual relationship. He is a cousin and a therapist. The potential for harm to the client exists and that is why this is considered unethical.

105. B: The best response to a client experiencing auditory hallucinations, saying "Don't you hear them?" is to state "I know the voices seem real to you, but I don't hear them." This response validates the client's perception and real fear of the voices ("I know the voices seem real to you") while orienting the client to reality ("I don't hear them"). The counselor should speak in a calm voice and avoid standing too close to or touching the client without permission as these actions may increase the client's fear and anxiety.

106. C: An EAP may be located within a company or outside of it when the company contracts with a provider. An EAP is an employee assistance program, not an educational assistance program. It is designed to help employees of a company get counseling if they need it, not to help college students. An EAP does employ licensed professional counselors to counsel employees who are referred for counseling by their employers.

107. C: John Holland based the SDS on the six different categories of personality types. He believed that individuals choose careers based on personality types and environmental influences. An individual's behavior is determined by the interaction between environment and personality.

108. B: If a client comes to a counselor with a problem with which he has very little experience or training, the ethical course of action is to refer the client to someone else who has the proper training and experience. Studying about a particular disorder may help the counselor to better understand the dynamics of the disorder, but it is no substitute for actual training and experience. Treating the man for something that is directly related to the problem he reports is not the standard of professional practice the counselor wants to avow.

109. A: Reliability involves consistency and equivalence. When a test is reliable, it is means that a test taker would receive nearly the same score every time the test taker would take the test. Another form of reliability is equivalence. A person who takes one form of a test would be expected to have nearly identical scores on another form of that test. Terms such as "concurrent" and "construct" refer to types of validity. "Stability" would be a term relating to reliability.

110. A: Group participants tend to take on different roles within the group, usually based upon how the individual interacts with others outside of the group. There are a number of different roles. Scapegoats generally take the blame for things that go wrong in the group. They allow others to point the finger at them without resistance. Placaters are the individuals in the group who try to

47

Copyright © Mometrix Media. You have been licensed one copy of this document for personal use only. Any other reproduction or redistribution is strictly prohibited. All rights reserved.

appease everyone. They usually are uncomfortable with any conflict and are easily drawn to making concessions to keep peace in the group. Dominators or monopolizers are those who seem to control the group's discussions. They steer the discussion in the direction they want it to go. They seldom allow others to talk. Jokers, on the other hand, are those who make light of things, usually as a defense. They typically lack confidence and use humor as a way to detract or distract others from conflictual situations.

111. D: A null hypothesis is one in which the researcher states prior to beginning the research that there will be no differences between groups and that if differences are found they will be due to chance and not due to being in one group or another. The research hypothesis states that there will be differences between the experimental and control groups and that the differences are due to something other than chance (i.e., the manipulation of the independent variable).

112. A: Conversion disorder (which is sometimes still referred to as hysterical neurosis) occurs when psychological stress is converted into a physical symptom. There must be no physical cause of the physical symptom for the diagnosis of conversion disorder to be made. Most of the time, physical symptoms will occur quite suddenly following a stressful event or experience. They can be as simple as a lump in the throat or as debilitating as a paralysis of a limb. The exact cause of conversion disorder is unknown, and treatment is often psychotherapy and stress management.

113. C: Reciprocity is a process whereby one credentialing agency (such as a state licensure board) accepts the credential of another agency (such as the licensure board for another state) as equivalent to its own license. It does not mean that one state licensure board actually grants licensure to a counselor who is licensed in another state, but rather that the first state licensure board would accept that counselor's license from the other state as being equivalent to its own license. Answers A and B do not involve licensure or credentialing at all.

114. C: A cognitive behavioral therapy (CBT) approach that focuses on relapse prevention for drug use disorders will likely help clients identify situations that make them vulnerable to relapse. Therapy may include training in behavioral skills and the use of cognitive interventions to assist them to identify triggers or situations that result in relapse as well as to provide tools they can use if faced with a situation that is placing the client at risk, such as when associates are engaging in addictive behavior.

115. C: A good strategy for helping a client overcome feelings of low self-esteem includes providing opportunities for the client to make decisions. Other strategies include providing companionship and listening and encouraging the client to express her feelings and concerns. Positive feedback and praise should be given when earned rather than praising everything. Telling the client that she has no reason to be depressed will invalidate her feelings and further lower her self-esteem. Low self-esteem is common among older adults because they have to deal with so many losses. They may become depressed, passive, and dependent.

116. D: The WISC is the Wechsler Intelligence Scale for Children, and it tests the intellectual ability of children from age six to sixteen. It was developed by David Wechsler and has gone through revisions since its origination. The test is commonly used today to determine intellectual impairment, or gifted status, for school-aged children. It is also used to determine the presence of neurological impairment. The test consists of several subtests in both "verbal" and "performance" categories, and provides scaled scores on the subtests, as well as an overall verbal IQ, performance IQ, and full-scale IQ score.

Copyright © Mometrix Media. You have been licensed one copy of this document for personal use only. Any other reproduction or redistribution is strictly prohibited. All rights reserved.

117. D: If utilizing dialectical behavioral therapy (DBT) to work with a small group of clients with borderline personality disorder, during the weekly group therapy session, one of the primary focuses is on improving interpersonal effectiveness. In the group, the clients can practice effective strategies and learn how to handle conflict. Other focuses include teaching mindfulness, distress tolerance skills, and regulation of emotions. In addition to group therapy, the clients should have individual weekly sessions during which they prioritize a list of problems, identify quality of life issues, and enhance self-image.

118. B: Sensate focus exercises are used to eliminate performance anxiety by instructing the couple to engage in touching that is non-sexual or non-erotic. The thought here is that if the couple can feel comfortable with touch, then sexual or erotic touch will not be as threatening.

119. D: If the counselor teaches a client with anxiety how to do relaxation exercises in order to relieve the anxiety, this is an example of reciprocal inhibition (AKA counterconditioning) because relaxation is incompatible with anxiety, so this incompatible response essentially cancels the undesirable one. This technique is utilized as part of behavioral therapy and often used with systematic desensitization to help clients reduce the fear response to exposure to things to which they have phobias.

120. A: Harry Harlow gave us a great understanding of human behavior through his experiments with rhesus monkeys. His famous experiments, using a wire/cloth "mother" monkey, were done to demonstrate the need for affection being greater than other needs, including the physical. Harlow's work was important not just for the obvious benefits of the research itself, but also for its long-reaching implications, which are used today for abused and neglected children, children who suffer from early losses in their lives, and other related issues. His work helped to shape how social service agencies, childcare workers, adoption agencies, and orphanages care for and manage children today.

121. D: Henry is displaying characteristics of the ego integrity stage. Erikson's ego integrity stage involves older adults who review their lives, looking at successes and regrets. Henry's age and his discussion about his life successes and regrets, not finding another mate, being successful in school, or contributing to society are examples of the thoughts that occur at this stage. Erikson's generativity stage involves middle-aged adults who are launching their children, dealing with an empty nest, and working toward retirement.

122. A: Co-leaders of different gender can actually be a strength in the group setting. Likewise, noting possible problems in potential members is not always an issue, as they can be used within the group dynamics to the enhancement of the group process. Having multiple opinions and perspectives allows for group members to gain perspective on their own issues and can be constructive in healing. A problem arises however, when firm goals are not set for the group. Depending upon the leader and members, it can be easy for the goals to be diluted if firm goals aren't set and adhered to at the start of the sessions. It takes a strong facilitator to keep the focus on the goals and move the group ahead.

Copyright © Mometrix Media. You have been licensed one copy of this document for personal use only. Any other reproduction or redistribution is strictly prohibited. All rights reserved.

123. C: Clanging. Thought patterns include:

Broadcasting	Clients believe that others can hear or understand their thoughts as though they are being broadcast.
Clanging	Clients' communication focuses on sounds, such as rhyme, "I want to tell, oh well, life is hell."
Derailment	Clients slip from one topic to another that is tangentially related or unrelated, "I saw the moon last night. . . . The late movie was exciting."
Loose association	Clients jump from one topic to another with little or no coherence. "The dog barks. The president sees a snake."

124. D: Antianxiety drugs are also sometimes called tranquilizers or benzodiazepines. They work by affecting the central nervous system, and have an overall calming effect on the client. They tend to be fast-acting, so can be useful for times of panic as well as for long-term anxiety issues. These medications work quite well for many clients, but there can be some negative side effects. Sleepiness, dizziness, and other such sedative-related side effects can make it difficult for some clients to effectively conduct their daily lives while medicated. Some commonly prescribed anti-anxiety drugs are alprazolam, diazepam, and lorazepam.

125. C: Vocational psychology is concerned with an individual's personality traits as they relate to vocation. It also explores issues such as development over the lifespan, working relationships with others, adaptations to the demands of work, choosing a vocation, and dysfunction. In recent years, interest has also been moving toward global issues. Vocational psychology also develops a variety of assessments (such as job satisfaction and description tests) and methods in relation to personality and vocational choice. Research and methods in vocational psychology are utilized by a variety of professionals, including counseling psychologists.

126. D: When working with a client with conduct disorder, limit setting includes (1) informing client of limits, (2) explaining the consequences of noncompliance, and (3) stating expected behaviors. Application of limit setting must be consistent and carried out by all staff members at all times. Consequences must be individualized and must have meaning for the client so that the client is motivated to avoid them. Negotiating a written agreement that can be referred to can prevent conflicts if the client tries to change the limits.

127. A: Erik Erikson essentially supports much of Sigmund Freud's theory, but is more socially and culturally oriented than Sigmund Freud was. Erikson extended beyond Freud's theory of development, theorizing eight separate psychological struggles that are critical to the development of the personality. He believed that there is evidence from as far back as primitive cultures of a belief in the unconscious. That's one of the reasons he felt one of Freud's greatest contributions to psychology was the idea of the unconscious and its role in the lives of individuals.

128. C: After action, belief, and the consequent affect, the remaining modalities are: 1) Disputing the belief that causes the affect (if it is irrational), and 2) the cognitive effect, which is defined as a change in the client's self-verbalization (evidencing understanding). According to Ellis, reconstructing one's irrational beliefs and self-talk will correct one's inappropriate feelings and behaviors.

129. D: All of these are tests routinely used in career counseling. The ITBS is an achievement test. Depending on the educational level, age, intelligence, and social and cultural background of the client, a career counselor might use the ITBS, SAT, Test of Adult Basic Education, ACT, GRE or a combination of several tests. The Myers-Briggs Type Indicator and MMPI are personality test. A

Copyright © Mometrix Media. You have been licensed one copy of this document for personal use only. Any other reproduction or redistribution is strictly prohibited. All rights reserved.

counselor can use personality testing to get a better idea of which occupations would be a good fit with a client's personality characteristics. The Minnesota Importance Questionnaire is a test of values (i.e., what is most important to an individual). Other values tests include the O*Net Work Importance Profiler and Super's Work Value Inventory (revised). A counselor could use values testing to ascertain what things are most important to a client, which would provide some direction in occupational choices.

130. B: Before beginning a counseling or therapy group, informed consent should be obtained. It requires the leader to provide adequate information to the prospective members about their rights and shared expectations, and it is complete only after the prospective members both understand and agree once they have been informed. Although maintaining confidentiality is an ethical obligation of group members, it CANNOT always be assured and group members must be informed of this. Leaders should also identify specific exceptions to confidentiality for the members (e.g., court orders, individual and community safety, etc.). In counseling or therapy groups, members are discouraged from forming outside social relationships and discussing group issues in such social groups. Members and leaders should agree on how they will deal with this if it does occur. In multicultural groups, the leader needs to model respect for cultural differences among the group members; it is not the responsibility of the members alone. Leaders may need to discuss their cultural values and assumptions early on within the group.

131. A: To investigate a particular test, best practice would be to read test critiques in books like Tests in Print or Buros Mental Measurements, read journal articles about that particular test, and test manuals. Online blogs may or may not utilize reliable information or sources, therefore are better to be avoided in instances of researching trends in testing and assessment.

132. D: Whether said in jest or not, it is the counselor's duty to assess lethality. The counselor needs to assess whether or not the client has a plan and a means to complete the act. The counselor could be held liable if he is negligent in assessing lethality. Any comments made about suicide must be taken seriously.

133. B: Type II error has an inverse relationship with significance level (i.e., it will increase as the significance level decreases). Type II error is wrongly accepting the null hypothesis that there is no significant difference. The lower the significance level, the more chance there is of this happening. Answer A is the reverse of the correct answer. Answer C is not true in that there is definitely a direct relationship between significance level and type II error. It is not true that the amount of type II error can go up or down as the significance level decreases.

134. C: Having business cards with "Dr." on them is misrepresentation, since the counselor has not received his doctoral degree. It does not matter that "Professional Counselor" was also on the business card. Clients who see "Dr." usually assume that the person has received a doctorate.

135. B: Maturational diagnosis is NOT one of Crites' three kinds of diagnoses. Crites is known for the idea of vocational maturity, but there is no "maturational" diagnosis in his approach. His three diagnoses are "differential", i.e., identifying what the problems are; "dynamic", i.e., identifying what has caused the problems; and, "decisional", i.e., identifying how the person is dealing with the problems.

136. C: Whitaker uses all of the techniques in this question except educating to promote change. The emphasis in symbolic family therapy is on shared experiences to promote change within families rather than education. Whitaker also believed that it is important to view the family as a

Copyright © Mometrix Media. You have been licensed one copy of this document for personal use only. Any other reproduction or redistribution is strictly prohibited. All rights reserved.

unit, so he emphasized families setting boundaries, developing a sense of who they are as families (family nationalism), and taking apart and rejoining the family.

137. D: In classical conditioning, an association is created between a stimulus that normally would not have a given autonomic effect on the animal and a stimulus that would. For example, a primary stimulus (such as food) evokes an involuntary response (such as salivation), or light evokes an involuntary contraction of the eye's pupil. During conditioning, a secondary stimulus, such as ringing a bell, is paired with the primary stimulus. With consistent repetition, the subject comes to associate the ringing bell with the involuntary response. Thus, when the primary stimulus of food or light is removed, the ringing bell alone evokes the same involuntary response of salivation or pupil contraction. In operant conditioning, an association is created between a behavior and a consequence. Thus, a positive stimulus presented following a voluntary response by the subject will reinforce or strengthen the recurrence of that response. For example, a child sits down and an adult praises the child. The child is then more likely to sit down again to receive praise. With repetition of reinforcement, the behavior will occur more often. Animals will also respond to operant condition. For example, they can learn that if they press a button or a lever, they will receive a food reward, and will thus repeat the behavior to obtain more food. The key difference is that in operant conditioning a voluntary response is evoked, while in classical conditioning an involuntary (autonomic) response is evoked.

138. B: There are three main types of conflict that can cause great stress. Approach/approach, avoidance/ avoidance, and approach/avoidance are the three types of conflict. In this case, the conflict is one of approach/avoidance. The client loves sweets, but yet also hates the sweets for what they cause to happen. So, in essence, the client approaches the source of conflict, and also avoids it. Avoidance/avoidance is when both circumstances are negative, yet one must be chosen. With approach/approach, the individual must choose between two positive situations.

139. A: Automatisms: Repeated behaviors that are without purpose, such as drumming fingers on the table and tapping the foot. **Psychomotor retardation**: Overall slowness in movement outside of what is normal. **Waxy flexibility**: Maintaining positions or postures over a period of time that appear awkward or uncomfortable. **Nervous tics**: Rapid, repetitive involuntary movements, such as eye twitching or blinking.

140. B: According to the Social Readjustment Rating Scale (Holmes and Rahe, 1967), marital issues, such as death of a spouse, divorce, and marital separation are the greatest stressors. Note that one positive, getting married, is also highly stressful. In descending order, other common stressors are being fired from a job, sexual dysfunction/difficulties, and change in living conditions. The Scale includes 43 major stressful life events, each assigned a score ranging from 100 (death of a spouse) to 11 (minor violations of the law). If a client scores less than 150, the client has a 30% chance of suffering from stress; and greater than 150, a 50% chance.

141. D: To better understand these concepts, it is important to recognize that inductive reasoning draws upon specific concepts in pursuing more general (i.e., generalizable) understandings and insights. By contrast, deductive reasoning draws upon overarching general understandings in pursuing specific insights. Thus, inductive research often leads to the building of theory. It also begins at the level of the real world and is practical in nature, so answer A is incorrect. By its nature, deductive research tends to come out of theory which already exists, so answer B is incorrect. In addition to predisposing theory formation, deductive research tends to be descriptive, correlational, and historical, so answer C is incorrect. Deductive research attempts to find relationships between the elements of a theory, and in doing so it often requires experimental research.

Copyright © Mometrix Media. You have been licensed one copy of this document for personal use only. Any other reproduction or redistribution is strictly prohibited. All rights reserved.

142. B: "Defense mechanism" is a term used in psychodynamic theory that refers to the unconscious distortions of reality that people make. A hypothesis is a hunch or assumption that a researcher starts with when designing a study. The researcher wants to verify whether or not this hunch or assumption is true. It is what the researcher is testing. It is not the conclusions that the researcher makes based on the data obtained.

143. B: If a counselor ends a discussion with the client about modifying the client's plan of care by saying, ""I understand you to say that you want to try some alternative treatments, such as imagery and relaxation, to help cope with your anxiety," this is an example of summarizing. With summarizing, it's important to accurately reflect the client's statements without judgment. Stating the summary verbally helps to verify that the counselor's understanding is correct and helps the client feels the client's ideas are validated.

144. B: 0.64, or 64% = 0.80², or 0.80 squared. The amount of true variance (versus error variance), is measured by the square of the correlation of the tests. Response A would be the correlation halved; response C would be 20% of the correlation; and response D would be the correlation with no change.

145. B: Measures of central tendency refer to the mean, median, and mode of any distribution. It describes "average" scores. In the bell curve, the measures of central tendency are those that are in the middle of the distribution. Stanines and percentiles are types of scores, and range and variance are related to measure of variability, not central tendency.

146. D: The suggested minimum sample sizes are a sample of at least 15 individuals for experimental and ex post facto research; a sample of at least 30 individuals for correlational research; and a sample of at least 100 individuals for survey research. Sample size influences statistical hypothesis testing. There are tables available for determining the appropriate sample size. In general, it is considered the rule that from 5% to 10% of the population is enough. The numbers suggested are a guideline for the smallest sample size to be selected for the respective types of studies as smaller numbers will not likely be representative nor give normal distributions.

147. D: Adler cited birth order and the family as major influences on individual development. Wolpe developed a theory of reciprocal inhibition, which states that anxiety and relaxation cannot simultaneously coexist. Only Wolpe used systematic desensitization—a behavioral intervention that creates counter-conditioning by pairing aversive stimuli with more pleasant ones. Adler did view neuroses as failures in learning that caused distorted perceptions, but he did not use behavioral techniques to change them. He emphasized client responsibility and a collaborative relationship in counseling. Carl Jung and Rollo May had in common their emphases on the existential concepts of identity, meaning, and purpose. Gordon Allport and Kurt Lewin both believed in systems: Allport saw human behavior as fitting within interactional systems such as cultures, situations, and field theory. Lewin was a field theorist who saw "life space" as a function of the individual and the environment, and behavior as a function of life space. Sigmund Freud and Aaron Beck were both psychoanalysts. Freud founded psychoanalysis and proposed the concepts of the conscious, the unconscious, and the preconscious. Beck was a neo-Freudian who identified "automatic thoughts" similar to Freud's preconscious.

148. C: If the counselor is conducting research on clients' level of health literacy based on scores on a questionnaire and plotting the scores on a curve to review the distribution, the counselor would expect 68% to fall within one standard deviation of the mean on a normal curve. The curve shows the distribution of all possible scores; but, in reality, data rarely fits so neatly into a curve and some skewing of data, such as to the right or left, may occur.

Copyright © Mometrix Media. You have been licensed one copy of this document for personal use only. Any other reproduction or redistribution is strictly prohibited. All rights reserved.

149. D: Family therapists are actively involved in the process. They are fairly structured and give homework assignments to families. They are generally flexible and go with the flow of the family. Oftentimes, family therapists "join" with families rather than keeping their distance.

150. C: The 20th percentile represents the twentieth element in the "distribution" of 100. In other words, it is the score at or below which 20% of the scores in the distribution fall. This does not reflect the quality of the score, but rather the relation of one's score to the rest in the distribution.

151. D: If a client with schizophrenia has shown structural brain abnormalities on cerebral CT and MRI, the client should suspect that the client will exhibit primarily negative symptoms. Clients with normal cerebral CTs and MRIs are more likely to exhibit positive symptoms (delusions, hallucinations, and disorganized thoughts, speech, and behavior) and tend to respond better to treatment than those with structural abnormalities. Examples of negative symptoms include flattening of affect, alogia (speech impairment), avolition, and apathy.

152. B: If a client with a history of schizophrenia and substance abuse appears in the office with disheveled appearance, disorganized behavior, thought distortion, and agitation and makes overt threats, the counselor's initial response should be to speak calmly and reassuringly and avoid sudden movement. The goal is to ensure safety of the counselor and client and to help to defuse the situation and calm the client so that emergency psychiatric stabilization can be carried out.

153. D: Clients with schizophrenia, depression, and bipolar disease are at high risk for dual diagnosis as many clients self-medicate with alcohol or illicit drugs. These clients often need enrollment in a program that targets both problems, as the approach to treatment for substance abuse is different for mentally ill clients than for those who are not mentally ill. Programs for dual diagnosis clients tend to be more supportive and less confrontational. Peer support is also important to treatment.

154. C: Meta-analysis is research that compares the results of many studies in order to answer one or more research questions. A quasi-experiment is similar to experimental research but subjects cannot be randomized into treatment and control groups. A survey uses questionnaires and/or interviews to measure the attitudes and perceptions of respondents. Comparative research investigates any differences between groups without manipulating the conditions for each group.

155. A: If a client has admitted to having fantasies about pedophilia and enjoying child pornography and the client justifies this interest by stating that children want to engage in sexual activity with adults, the approach to cognitive therapy that is most indicated is cognitive restructuring. Cognitive restructuring is a method to change the way in which clients think about something. The client is provided information about how thoughts can affect behavior and helped to correct these thought patterns in order to differentiate between appropriate and inappropriate thoughts.

156. B: Integrity versus despair is one of the stages in Erickson's psychosocial developmental theory. Kohlberg postulated that in the first level, preconventional, individuals are concerned with consequences imposed upon them for wrongdoing. Thus, in the example, Cody wanted to avoid being punished by having his television privileges taken away. At the conventional level, an individual wants to conform to societal rules so that authority rules and order is maintained. At the postconventional level, individuals define morality in terms of universal values and altruism.

157. B: Sigmund Freud outlined several defense mechanisms. These defense mechanisms are ways that the Ego can defend against levels of anxiety that have become too intense to manage. There are several defense mechanisms, but one of the more commonly referred to is repression. Anna Freud

Copyright © Mometrix Media. You have been licensed one copy of this document for personal use only. Any other reproduction or redistribution is strictly prohibited. All rights reserved.

referred to repression as "motivated forgetting," which is a rather clear description of the mechanism. Quite simply, if something is too stressful to deal with, the Ego represses it (forgets it), in order to manage the anxiety. It's important to note that repressed memories do not disappear, but are simply in a type of storage, awaiting retrieval.

158. D: Extinction is a behavioral technique of ignoring a behavior until the individual or group stops engaging in it. This is useful if the sole purpose of the behavior is to seek attention. Deprived of reinforcement (attention) long enough, the person(s) is/are likely to abandon their attention-seeking behaviors. However, in a group setting, ignoring a resistant behavior is not usually effective. (It might work with certain attention-seeking behaviors, such as talking too much or too loudly, interrupting, etc., but it would be unlikely to help in situations of resistance in the form of silence even if it is attention-seeking.) Confrontation has been identified as a powerful technique for dealing with resistance. Group leaders modeling ways to deal with resistance can also be effective. Discussion of resistive behaviors with the group before they occur is often a good way to prevent them.

159. A: The "self-fulfilling prophecy" is attributed to the sociologist Robert Merton in his book Social Theory and Social Structure. The idea is that the act of predicting something (even though not true at the time of the prediction) can make it eventually come true. Behavior as a result of the false prediction begins to change because of it, and to be seen as proof of it actually being true, which the prediction eventually becomes. For example, telling a teacher that a particular student is gifted may cause her to behave differently toward him (enhanced attention and reinforcement perhaps), which may eventually lead to the student performing better than he would have. Thus, the false prediction becomes true.

160. C: If a client with intellectual disability has moved into an assisted living facility but has had trouble adjusting and making new friends, resulting in increasing isolation and depression, the technique that is likely to be most effective in working with this client is role paying and modeling because these techniques are concrete and help the client to practice interactions. Interventions should be specific rather than general and avoid the need for abstract thinking and insight, which may be difficult for the client.

161. A: EMDR stands for the experimental counseling technique called eye movement desensitization and reprocessing. It is used to help the client to access memories of traumatic experiences and to reprocess those experiences via rapid eye movements (REM) similar to those seen during REM phases of sleep. This is when the sleeper is thought to be dreaming or otherwise processing mental images. Answers B, C, and D are all phrases made up to fit the initials.

162. D: Social Identity Theory basically says that when individuals belong or are assigned to a group, they tend to think of that group as elite or special. People want to have a positive self-image, so identifying themselves with the elite group makes them feel they are better than others. Social Identity theory is attributed to Henry Tajfel. Tajfel's theory is used to explain conflict and prejudice between groups. He was a European Jew who survived World War II, and his theory developed out of his attempts to explain the violence he had experienced as a part of his "group."

163. B: The Minnesota Multiphasic Personality Inventory (MMPI) is one of the most researched psychological tests. It was developed in the 1930s by Starke R. Hathaway and J.C. McKinley at the University of Minnesota, and an updated version (MMPI-2) was released in 1989. The MMPI is used for a variety of reasons, including in the criminal justice system, for determining suitability in some professions, and in child custody cases. However, it is most often used in determining psychological disorders. The test consists of ten scales, each focusing on a particular psychological disorder.

Copyright © Mometrix Media. You have been licensed one copy of this document for personal use only. Any other reproduction or redistribution is strictly prohibited. All rights reserved.

There are also validity scales to highlight when a client is lying, or trying to influence the score one way or another, and other safeguards to aid in the interpretation of the results.

164. A: Mentor, employer, and advisor are NOT roles defined by Super. The nine life roles he identified are: child, student, citizen, spouse, homemaker, parent, worker, leisurite, and pensioner. Super's theory is developmental and holistic. He formulated the concept of the "life-career rainbow," which encompassed his major stages of the life span and the life space (drawn from his interpretation these roles).

165. B: The Social Learning Theory of Career Decision-Making, as it was first called by Mitchell and Krumboltz, was later developed into the Learning Theory of Career Counseling (LTCC). Its basic foundation is Albert Bandura's Social Learning Theory as it seeks to explain why people make the choices they do in relation to careers. Some influences on an individual's career choice are environmental conditions, associative learning, and genetic endowment. The LTCC also has the practical application of guiding counselors in dealing the problems that can arise from those choices.

166. D: Bowen applied his theory of families to the emotional functioning of society as well. His concept of societal regression expressed his belief that society is moving backwards, because it fails to differentiate between emotional decision-making and intellectual decision making. Bowen stated that the basic building block of a family's emotional system is a triangle not a quadrangle. What Bowen called the differential of self refers to the degree to which individuals can distinguish between their thought processes and their emotional processes not between self and others. In the nuclear family emotional system, Bowen said people choose marital partners with equal levels of differentiation to their own; if partners are undifferentiated, they will produce similarly undifferentiated family members resulting in an unstable system, not a more stable one.

167. A: Random sampling is a very basic form of probability sampling and is commonly known. It involves samples being drawn from a population in which the entire population has an equal chance of being chosen for the sample. Usually each element from the population is selected only once ("without replacement"), but sometimes the item may be returned to the population and has the chance of being selected once again. Random sampling seems very simple in theory, but can be difficult because all of the elements of the population must be identified first before they can be sampled.

168. B: In a client-centered group, the leader points out feelings, personal meanings, and individual attitudes. The function of this type of group is to increase self-understanding and altering of self-concepts. In a transactional analysis group, the leader focuses on life scripts and the dynamic ego states of parent, adult, and child and how these dynamic ego states impact others. In an encounter group, the leader focuses on the development of the individual, emotional experiences, and awareness of the behavior of others. A leader of a psychoanalytic group attempts to re-create, analyze, and interpret the participants' defenses, resistances, and transferences.

169. A: Whenever a counselor is going to begin a therapy group, she must screen all of the possible clients to make sure that they are good candidates for group therapy. She does not need to diagnose each client. Allowing the clients to try the group before committing to it really hampers the group process. An interview indicates an overly excessive method of assessing suitability.

170. C: In milieu therapy (AKA therapeutic community), if a person exhibits inappropriate behavior, the correct response is to help the client examine the effect the behavior has on others and to discuss more appropriate ways of behaving. With milieu therapy, expectations are that all

Copyright © Mometrix Media. You have been licensed one copy of this document for personal use only. Any other reproduction or redistribution is strictly prohibited. All rights reserved.

clients can grow and that all interactions have the potential to be therapeutic. Clients "own" their environment and behavior and must be responsible for both. Peer pressure is used to provide direct feedback, and consequences (punishment/restrictions) are to be avoided.

171. B: The authoritarian parenting style uses coercive techniques and psychological control to discipline children, whereas the authoritative parenting style emphasizes some control but allows for some independence. The uninvolved parenting style rarely uses any control and the parent seems to be indifferent to the child's level of independence. In the permissive parenting style, the parents are typically overindulgent with the child. They exert very little control and are lenient when it comes to granting independence to the child.

172. A: Triangulation and "enmeshment" are two common terms in family therapy. The family power structure is out of balance, but what is happening is that some of the family members are forming an unhealthy coalition against another family member, which is considered triangulation. Enmeshment occurs when there is diffusion of boundaries. There are intrusions where none should be made. It is as if one member of the family were trying to live through another member of that family.

173. C: If a 7-year-old child with autism spectrum disorder refuses to eat any foods or drinks other than one specific brand of crackers and apple juice. has begun to develop nutritional deficiencies and weight loss, and throws a tantrum if the parents attempt to provide other food or drinks, the most likely diagnosis is avoidant/restrictive food intake disorder. Rigid eating habits are common in those with ASD but should not result in nutritional deficiencies or require treatment.

174. D: The "validity" of a test tells how useful it will be, or in other words, if the test is accurately measuring what one wants it to measure. When speaking of validity in testing, several types of validity are often referred to. "Construct validity" is how well the test measures the "construct" that it was designed to measure. In "concurrent validity," "convergent validity" tells one whether or not the test will give results similar to other tests like it, and "divergent validity" will reveal if the test gives different results from tests that measure different constructs. Any particular construct consists of a number of factors that must be taken into account, and a test's "content validity" tells one if the test takes those factors into consideration. Finally, "criterion-related validity" refers to the test's ability to predict the client's performance.

175. D: In observational research, the results can be biased by the measurement itself. The "observer effect" is a type of measurement effect. It refers to the subjects in the research study behaving differently because they know they are being observed. The Hawthorne effect came about as a result of a workplace study near Chicago in the 1950s, and the term was coined by Henry Landsberger. A study had been commissioned to determine if workers would be more productive in more light or less light. The study showed that light levels didn't matter because simply knowing they were being studied caused the employees to work harder.

176. C: The goal of the harm-reduction based model of recovery from substance abuse is to use substances more responsibly rather than abstinence, which is unattainable for some clients. This model focuses on teaching clients about the negative consequences of substance abuse and guiding them to carry out other methods to reduce risks, such as choosing different drugs and altering the pattern of use or other behaviors, such by using a designated driver rather than driving after drinking. This model is often used with legal drugs, such as alcohol, prescription drugs, and marijuana (in some states).

Copyright © Mometrix Media. You have been licensed one copy of this document for personal use only. Any other reproduction or redistribution is strictly prohibited. All rights reserved.

177. A: A norm is NOT a measure of central tendency. A norm refers to a typical behavior or an established standard of conduct. It may, however, be expressed by means of statistical averages. In group therapy, a norm is a written or unwritten rule of conduct or behavior. The mean is the arithmetic average of the scores or measurements of a number of individuals, and thus it is a measure of central tendency. The median is the middle score in a distribution of scores and is also a measure of central tendency. The mode is the most frequent score in a distribution and is another measure of central tendency.

178. C: In all of the therapies named, the goal is to make changes in the family's functioning, and in all of them the counselor takes an active role by interacting directly with the family. Strategic family therapy (Jay Haley, Cloe Madanes) has the goal of perceiving the existing situation differently (relabeling), and Murray Bowen, the creator of family systems theory, preferred taking a neutral position as a counselor. Maintaining the balance of the family system is a goal of Milan systemic family therapy, and counselors will most often have the role of a trainer in behavioral approaches to family therapy. Counselors in strategic family therapy often have teacher-like roles as their techniques include giving clients assignments. Social constructionist family therapy has the goal of helping the family to use the knowledge it already possesses. The social constructionist theory gave rise to de Shazer's and O'Hanlon's solution-based therapeutic approaches.

179. B: In seeking to determine causal relationships between variables, experimental research uses experimental groups (receiving an intervention or treatment) and control groups (receiving no intervention or treatment) to ensure that any observed changes are actually caused by the experimental treatment and not by some other intervening variable(s). Ideally all relevant factors in both groups should be being essentially equal except for the experimental treatment or intervention. Random subject assignment to either group helps ensure equivalent composition in each group in order to avoid biasing the results. Answers A, C, and D (survey research design, correlational research design, and descriptive research design) are all characteristics of non-experimental research designs.

180. B: A neutral stimulus remains a neutral stimulus unless it can be associated with something that already elicits some sort of response. If a stimulus that already elicits a response is presented first, the response has already occurred. The neutral stimulus coming after the unconditioned stimulus (US) does nothing because the response has already occurred. Therefore, the neutral stimulus must be presented before the US so that it becomes associated with the US and can then evoke a response similar to the unconditioned response. Although simultaneous occurrence with the US would evoke a conditioned response, in everyday life two things do not get presented at the exact same time very often. Presenting a neutral stimulus at random will not allow for any association to be made between it and the US.

181. C: If something is confounded, it is confusing or befuddling. Therefore, when looking at research, if variables cannot be distinguished or the result cannot clearly be attributed to the independent or dependent variable, then a study is confounded. This is generally caused by external influences that were not accounted for or controlled. Confounding variables can discount experiment results.

182. B: Outsourcing is when a company takes jobs that would have traditionally been done in-house, and contracts with another company to have them done from somewhere else. Companies increasingly outsource jobs because it can save them money in overhead expenses and benefits, and it usually costs less to get the job done than if they did it with an in-house employee. Outsourcing can also save in time for management as the outsourced jobs are managed by the contracted company. Disadvantages to the company are control and communication. For the employee,

Copyright © Mometrix Media. You have been licensed one copy of this document for personal use only. Any other reproduction or redistribution is strictly prohibited. All rights reserved.

outsourcing can be viewed as negative if one's job is eliminated because of it or positive if one is with the contracted company.

183. A: If a client with multiple sclerosis tells the counselor that she is upset that she can no longer continue her employment because her job is too physically demanding and is concerned about how she will support herself, the response that focuses on problem solving as a response to stress is "What plans do you have for finding a new job?" This response doesn't suggest a solution, such as public assistance, but indirectly suggests that the client can take control to solve the problem of work.

184. B: The personal belief system of the counselor, when engaging in a therapeutic relationship with a client, should not be an issue in therapy. The counselor should be fully aware of his/her belief system and how he/she may diverge from the beliefs of the client in order to keep them in proper perspective. The counselor must avoid allowing those beliefs to impact the counseling process. The focus should be upon the client, and his/her values and belief systems, with a constant respect for individual diversity.

185. A: The coefficient of determination equals the degree of common variance, or the square of the correlation. The coefficient of non-determination is the unique, or error variance, or the variance that is not in common (i.e., the difference between 100 minus the coefficient of determination. If the correlation were .80, the common variance (coefficient of determination) would be 64%, and the error variance (unique variance/coefficient of non-determination) would be 36%. Answer B is the opposite of the correct answer. Answers B and C are also opposites or reversed statements. Answer D is wrong because it is the correlation squared, not the correlation, which equals the coefficient of determination/common variance, and likewise the coefficient of non-determination/error variance is the difference between 100% and the square of the correlation, not the correlation.

186. B: A frequency distribution presents data in a way that one can see how often a particular value occurs. Likewise, in a grouped frequency distribution, groups of items or categories are shown. There commonly are also cumulative frequency distributions that address a set of data. The frequency distribution is important because it's a way to organize and make sense of a multitude of data. Some common ways to present the data in a frequency distribution is through a bar graph, frequency polygon, and a frequency curve.

187. B: Specification = age 18-21. Super defined five vocational developmental tasks during different age periods: crystallization, from age 14-18; specification, from age 18-21; implementation, from age 21-24; stabilization, from age 24-35; and consolidation, from age 35 onward. (Note: Super's ages no longer apply, as they were originally based mostly on middle-class, white, college-educated males, and because people now more often have gaps and/or changes in their careers.)

188. A: If an adolescent male client has become obsessed with body building and has been taking anabolic steroids and lifting weights so much that it has resulted in dangerous hypertension and muscle strain, and the client that he has to build muscle because he looks weak and small, the most likely diagnosis is muscle dysmorphia, a form of body dysmorphic disorder. This disorder occurs almost exclusively in males and involves excessive exercise, weight lifting, and diet as well as use of anabolic steroids even though severe health problems may result.

189. A: According to Freud, the oral stage is from birth to 18 months; the anal stage is from 2 to 3 years; the phallic stage is from 3 to 5 years; the latency stage is from 6 to 12 years; and the genital stage is from 12 to 19 years of age. The infant's psychosexual focus is on the mouth as it nurses to

Copyright © Mometrix Media. You have been licensed one copy of this document for personal use only. Any other reproduction or redistribution is strictly prohibited. All rights reserved.

obtain nourishment. The toddler's psychosexual focus moves to the anal area during toilet training as the child learns to control bowel movements. The early childhood psychosexual focus is on the phallus (the penis in males and the clitoris in females) as the child discovers his or her sexual organs. In middle childhood, the focus is on socialization, and Freud believed that children repress sexual urges until puberty. In adolescence, Freud said the psychosexual focus is on the genitals as sexual urges resurface and gain strength, and sexual activity begins.

190. B: "Conforming; swarming" is the one NOT written by Tuckman. The others refer to: 1) the formation of the group, or "forming"; 2) the processing and resolution of conflicts, or "storming"; 3) the process of conforming or not conforming to the group's norms, i.e., norming; 4) each member's participation and self-expression within the group and bonding with the group, i.e., performing; and 5) the termination of the group, i.e., mourning or adjourning.

191. B: Autocratic is NOT a common role for a group member; it is a leadership style used by some group leaders. Facilitative, maintenance and blocking are common roles for group members. A facilitative or building role is one wherein group members feel they contribute to the positive functioning of the group. A maintenance role contributes to the group by encouraging social and emotional bonding among members. A blocking role can hinder a group's attainment of goals by using negative or distracting behaviors.

192. B: While anxiety is certainly present, agoraphobia is more likely the culprit, given the client's feelings of unease while outside the home, and his relative ease while in the home setting. The agoraphobic individual experiences negative physical, psychological, and emotional symptoms when outside his comfort zone (which is often the home setting). In some cases, the symptoms are so severe that the client remains homebound for years, which can lead to secondary difficulties such as relationship and financial problems. The causes of agoraphobia are likely a combination of factors, which are varied. Several treatments are effective, but behavioral techniques, or a combined treatment modality, are likely to be most often utilized.

193. B: Undecided means that the person needs more information before making a decision; it refers to a state of being. Being indecisive, by contrast, is a personality trait. An indecisive person may be given all the information there is on a subject, and may still be unable to decide. With indecisive clients, personal counseling may be needed before career counseling can be effective. Answer A is untrue since undecided and indecisive are not synonyms. Answers C and D are opposites of the correct definitions.

194. A: If a client has been diagnosed with fetishistic disorder and has court-ordered therapy after an arrest for stealing women's undergarments, the best focus of the therapy may be on ways in which the client can find legal access to women's undergarments, such as by buying them (clean or soiled). Changing fetishistic behavior can be very difficult, especially if the client is not motivated to change and only receives sexual gratification with the item associated with the fetish, even if the fetish interferes with normal relationships, although some may benefit from CBT to lessen their response to the item.

195. C: If a counselor recognizes a personal bias against a particular ethnic/cultural group, the first step in mitigating the negative effects is to identify the nature of the bias, describe it, and consider

Copyright © Mometrix Media. You have been licensed one copy of this document for personal use only. Any other reproduction or redistribution is strictly prohibited. All rights reserved.

the cause. The counselor should try to identify how long the bias has been held and contributing factors as well as the possibility of a change in attitude. Subsequent steps include:

- List and try to comprehend the negative effects of the bias.
- Identify a number of strategies to deal with the bias.
- Determine the lessons learned from dealing with the bias.

196. D: If a client experiences a panic attack and thinks, "I can control this. I am just anxious, but the symptoms will go away if I remain calm," this is an example of positive reframing, which is a technique that is part of cognitive behavioral therapy and used to turn a negative thought or response into a positive one. Clients are encouraged to develop positive reframing messages in advance to cope with stress and even to write them down if necessary so that they are prepared when a stressful event occurs.

197. B: Humanistic psychology is often known as the "third force" in psychology because it came after psychoanalytic theory and behaviorism. Its founders are usually identified as Rollo May, Abraham Maslow, and Carl Rogers. It is also viewed as having its roots in existentialist thought, because it addresses not just illness, but the meaning of human existence. Humanistic psychology defined itself as different from psychoanalysis and behaviorism by its focus on helping the individual to achieve full potential. Psychoanalysis and behaviorism focused on problems and the elimination of those problems in the individual, but humanistic psychology moved beyond that to do more than simply alleviate problems and focus on the healthy aspects of the individual.

198. A: Leon Festinger, a social psychologist, developed the concept of cognitive dissonance. It refers to an individual's desire to avoid inconsistency and always move toward consistency. For example, when a man behaves in a manner that is inconsistent with his belief system, he will feel anxiety and seek to eliminate, or minimize, that anxiety. He will either seek to change his behavior, or come up with some reasons to justify his behavior. Those reasons, while not changing the original cause of the anxiety, will serve to at least help him to feel better about his behavior.

199. D: The SEM is calculated in advance, NOT after, the test is taken. It also may be reported on the test's score profile. The SEM is useful for interpreting an individual's test scores. It helps to determine the range within which an individual's test score is likely to fall. Finally, each test does have its own unique SEM value.

200. C: One of the techniques of Gestalt therapy is role playing. Since Gestalt therapy stresses the importance of facing feelings, role playing is an effective way to explore and express feelings toward another without their actual presence. In role playing, the counselor acts the part of someone the client is in conflict with, providing the client with the opportunity to say and do what they would want to if the person were really present. Sometimes the roles will be reversed in role playing as well, depending upon the needs of the situation. Role playing is a way to deal with feelings in a positive manner, with an ultimate goal of ensuring that feelings do not control the individual.

Copyright © Mometrix Media. You have been licensed one copy of this document for personal use only. Any other reproduction or redistribution is strictly prohibited. All rights reserved.

Practice Test #2

1. The test created by David Wechsler is what type of test?

    a. IQ
    b. Personality
    c. Developmental
    d. Functional

2. Carl Jung believed that teleology must be considered in understanding personality. What does teleology refer to?

    a. Goals
    b. The past
    c. The present
    d. Early childhood development

3. Terry's average score per basketball game is 27 points. This places him sixth among all the forwards in the Midwest basketball league. The level of measurement described in this example is:

    a. ordinal.
    b. ratio.
    c. interval.
    d. nominal.

4. What is the difference between confidentiality and privileged communication?

    a. Confidentiality is a legal concept, and privileged communication is an ethical concept
    b. Confidentiality is an ethical concept, and privileged communication is a legal concept
    c. Confidentiality and privileged communication are both legal and are the same thing
    d. Confidentiality and privileged communication are ethical concepts and are the same

5. Which of the following are examples of negative symptoms associated with schizophrenia?

    a. Hallucinations and delusions
    b. Inappropriate clothing, aggressive behavior, stereotyped behavior
    c. Abnormal though processes and speech patterns
    d. Blunt or flat affect, avolition, and reduced speech

6. A counselor with several clients is also adjusting to a difficult divorce. The counselor is not sleeping or eating well, is highly distractible, and is generally less in-touch with her emotional state. The counselor should:

    a. continue to see clients as she regularly would.
    b. discontinue client contact until she has adjusted to her new life situation.
    c. seek psychological help for herself.
    d. be alert to her mental status and be able to determine if continuing with her clients poses any threat of being detrimental to the counseling process.

Copyright © Mometrix Media. You have been licensed one copy of this document for personal use only. Any other reproduction or redistribution is strictly prohibited. All rights reserved.

7. Why did R. K. Conyne create the "Group Work Grid"?

a. To address psychotic issues among group members
b. To expand practical understanding of group work
c. In hopes of eliminating intergroup resistance issues
d. To clarify working relationships between group members

8. As of the 21st century, the number of certified and licensed counselors in the U.S. is close to:

a. 10,000.
b. 50,000.
c. 100,000.
d. 1,000,000.

9. Which of these is correct about insurance laws related to counseling?

a. In some states, insurance laws now require licensed counselors to be reimbursed for treating certain mental illnesses
b. Insurance laws in all states now require that licensed counselors be reimbursed for treating certain mental illnesses
c. There is no law in any state of the U.S. requiring insurance companies to reimburse licensed counselors
d. Insurance laws in all states now require insurance companies to reimburse licensed counselors for all mental illnesses

10. Robert Carkhuff categorized counselors' responses as all EXCEPT which one of the following?

a. Additive
b. Interchangeable
c. Subtractive
d. Multiplicative

11. Which of the following is a good example of a standardized test?

a. A checklist
b. A rating scale
c. A structured, scored test
d. An open-ended interview

12. Jason is a computer programmer. He is an excellent engineer but is not good at technical support, because he doesn't know how to converse easily with people. His wife, Sallie, is a teacher and she is great at explaining things. Children and others love her. However, she can never get her computer to work. John Holland would identify Jason and Sallie respectively as which of his six personality types or styles?

a. Jason is mainly a realistic type and Sallie is mainly an artistic type
b. Jason is mainly an investigative type and Sallie is mainly a social type
c. Jason is mainly a conventional type and Sallie is mainly an enterprising type
d. Jason is mainly an enterprising type and Sallie is mainly a conventional type

Copyright © Mometrix Media. You have been licensed one copy of this document for personal use only. Any other reproduction or redistribution is strictly prohibited. All rights reserved.

13. Interpersonal therapy is generally most effective for which of the following?

    a. Depressive episodes associated with specific situations
    b. Major depressive episodes
    c. Depressive episodes associated with bipolar disorder
    d. Depressive episodes associated with PTSD

14. Premature termination of participation in a group usually occurs when an individual is:

    a. not very motivated.
    b. highly intelligent.
    c. open to experiences.
    d. empathetic.

15. Dr. Stanwyck has determined that his two groups of students have significantly different scores on the post-test of self-efficacy he gave to them after two different courses of counseling. Now he wants to find out whether there is also a statistically significant interaction between the two groups' mean scores. What kind of test would he be likely to use to determine this?

    a. A one-way ANOVA
    b. A factorial ANOVA
    c. A MANOVA
    d. An ANCOVA

16. Styles of group leadership have been described as all EXCEPT:

    a. autocratic.
    b. effective.
    c. democratic.
    d. laissez faire.

17. A 20-year-old male college student has been referred for evaluation by his family. They note that over the last six to seven months he has increasingly avoided contact and/or talking with family members and friends, that he often seems intensely preoccupied, and that his hygiene and grooming have become very poor. In speaking with him the counselor notes that he seems very guarded, that his affect is virtually expressionless, and that he resists talking. When able to coax him to speak, his speech is very tangential, disorganized, and even incoherent at times. He seems to be responding to internal stimuli (hallucinations and/or intrusive thoughts). The family and he deny substance abuse. Which would be the MOST likely diagnosis?

    a. Schizophrenia
    b. Somatization disorder
    c. Bipolar disorder
    d. Major depression with psychotic features

18. Josie likes to play peek-a-boo with her little brother, Jack. According to Piaget, Jack finds this game fun because he has acquired _____, which is one of the primary tasks of the sensorimotor stage of cognitive development.

    a. conservation
    b. dual representation
    c. object permanence
    d. reversibility

Copyright © Mometrix Media. You have been licensed one copy of this document for personal use only. Any other reproduction or redistribution is strictly prohibited. All rights reserved.

19. True variance or the coefficient of determination is obtained by:

a. subtracting the correlation coefficient from 1.00.
b. adding the correlation coefficient to 1.00.
c. squaring the correlation coefficient.
d. none of the above.

20. A scatter plot depicts:

a. a multitude of single scores.
b. pairs of scores.
c. one score.
d. the unscored results of an experiment.

21. An appropriate primary intervention for clients at risk of emotional illness resulting from trauma, such as an act of violence, is to do which of the following?

a. Clarify the client's problem
b. Refer for inpatient treatment
c. Provide behavioral modification therapy
d. Institute a suicide prevention plan

22. Working with individuals from different cultures requires that the counselor do all the following EXCEPT:

a. have sensitivity to the needs of the individuals.
b. make a referral to another counselor.
c. have knowledge about the different cultures.
d. consider utilizing an interpreter if language differences are also present.

23. Which two psychologists most emphasize freedom of choice and responsibility in their theories?

a. B.F.   Skinner and Arnold Lazarus
b. William Glasser and Rollo May
c. Carl Rogers and Heinz Kohut
d. Albert Ellis and Eric Berne

24. Jennifer has to choose between spending the evening with her parents or spending the evening babysitting her younger sister. Jennifer does not like either of these choices. This situation describes an:

a. approach-avoidance conflict.
b. avoidance-avoidance conflict.
c. approach-approach conflict.
d. avoidance vector.

Copyright © Mometrix Media. You have been licensed one copy of this document for personal use only. Any other reproduction or redistribution is strictly prohibited. All rights reserved.

25. A 22-year old college student comes for counseling following a visit to a hospital emergency room where he was complaining of chest pain. The medical work-up was negative. During the counseling session the counselor learns that his father recently died of a heart attack (a few weeks ago) while he was away at school, and that he is now experiencing episodes of sudden-onset fear accompanied by symptoms such as a rapid heart rate, sweating, tremors, chest pain, and shortness of breath, and feelings that he is about to die. After a short time, the symptoms subside. In recent days he has been sleeping outside the hospital, fearful that he may not otherwise arrive in time when the symptoms strike. Which is the most likely diagnosis?

   a. Generalized anxiety disorder
   b. Panic disorder
   c. Somatization disorder
   d. Post-traumatic stress disorder

26. What is John Bowlby best known for?

   a. Psychosocial development theory
   b. Behavioral therapy
   c. The Oedipus complex
   d. Attachment theory

27. Negative reinforcement _____ the behavior by _____ a reinforcer; positive reinforcement _____ the behavior by _____ a reinforcer.

   a. increases, taking away; increases, adding
   b. increases, adding; increases, taking away
   c. decreases, adding; increases, adding
   d. decreases, taking away; increases, taking away

28. A t-score has a mean of _____ and a standard deviation of _____.

   a. 100; 15.
   b. 10; 2.
   c. 50; 15.
   d. 50; 10.

29. Jeremy is a counselor. He believes in mirroring back his client's verbalizations, and not passing judgment on what they say. Jeremy considers himself a facilitator in assisting his client in reaching resolution of the presenting problems. What type of therapeutic theory is Jeremy working from?

   a. Freudian psychoanalysis
   b. Behavioral theory
   c. Rogerian, client-centered therapy
   d. Jung's client-guiding theory

30. A 10-year-old boy refuses to eat at the dinner table with the rest of the family and often stays home when the family goes to the zoo or a museum. According to Minuchin, this youngster is _____ the family.

   a. disengaged from
   b. enmeshed in
   c. the placater in
   d. triangulated in

66

Copyright © Mometrix Media. You have been licensed one copy of this document for personal use only. Any other reproduction or redistribution is strictly prohibited. All rights reserved.

31. When working with prospective employers about hiring those with mental disabilities, an employer asks the counselor if it is legal to ask potential employees if they are disabled during the initial interview. Which of the following is the best response?

a. "Yes, you can ask if the person has a disability that may affect the job."
b. "You can ask if the person has any disability."
c. "You may ask only if the person can perform job functions."
d. "You may ask only if there are job-related functions the person cannot do."

32. A client in a support group assumes that another member of the group who is hearing impaired is also intellectually disabled. Which of the following is the correct description of this attitude?

a. Halo effect
b. Guilt by association
c. Disability as punishment
d. Attribution of responsibility

33. A counselor is conducting the initial screening of individuals who may be included in a bereavement group. An appropriate candidate for the group would be one who:

a. has a severe mental illness.
b. lacks cognitive and thinking abilities.
c. is free from the use of alcohol or other drugs.
d. has a history of violence or uncontrolled anger.

34. A malpractice claim can be lodged against a counselor when:

a. the counselor was negligent.
b. the client suffered physical or psychological injury.
c. a professional relationship was established.
d. All of the above.

35. Which of the following pairs of personality theorists and perspectives is INCORRECT?

a. Abraham Maslow; existentialist
b. Carl Rogers; humanist
c. Carl Jung; genetic
d. Sigmund Freud; psychodynamic

36. The Rorschach, TAT, and Rotters Incomplete Sentences are all:

a. projective tests.
b. observational tests.
c. rating scales.
d. standardized personality tests.

37. B.F. Skinner believed that punishment was:

a. a very effective technique in behavior modification.
b. counterproductive in behavior modification.
c. central to behavior modification.
d. better used as a last option in behavior modification.

Copyright © Mometrix Media. You have been licensed one copy of this document for personal use only. Any other reproduction or redistribution is strictly prohibited. All rights reserved.

38. Who developed the "social distance scale"?

    a.   Eric Berne
    b.   Avery Ellis
    c.   Emory Bogardus
    d.   Albert Bandura

39. Jim decides to go for counseling and makes an appointment. When he gets there, the counselor gives him a statement of disclosure. Which is true regarding this document?

    a.   A statement of disclosure is required by law in every state in the United States
    b.   A statement of disclosure is never required by law, but is highly recommended
    c.   A statement of disclosure may be required by law in some states and not others
    d.   A statement of disclosure should be given to a client after a course of therapy

40. Ethical dilemmas often center on issues related to:

    a.   dual relationships.
    b.   confidentiality.
    c.   credentials of test administrators.
    d.   licensure.

41. The Code of Ethics is:

    a.   legal and binding.
    b.   a hard and fast set of rules.
    c.   a set of standards of best practice.
    d.   All of the above.

42. What are some examples of culture-bound values vs. class-bound values in counseling?

    a.   Culture-bound values include strict adherence to a time schedule and an unstructured approach
    b.   Class-bound values include verbal expression, defined patterns of communication, and openness
    c.   Culture-bound values include individual-centered counseling, emotional expression, and intimacy
    d.   Class-bound values include a structured approach to problems and seeking short-term solutions

43. A counselor who has a current caseload of 124 clients decides to close his practice and move to Florida. Unethical handling of this change includes:

    a.   notifying all his clients in writing of his plans.
    b.   making referrals to other professionals for all of his clients.
    c.   safeguarding all client records.
    d.   calling patients to notify them of this change.

44. Which of the following screening tools for alcohol abuse include questions about socioeconomic status and psychological needs as well as the use of addictive substances?

    a.   CAGE (alcohol abuse tool)
    b.   Alcohol Use Disorders Identification Test (Modified) (AUDIT-C)
    c.   Addiction Severity Index (ASI)
    d.   Alcohol Use Disorders Identification Test (AUDIT)

Copyright © Mometrix Media. You have been licensed one copy of this document for personal use only. Any other reproduction or redistribution is strictly prohibited. All rights reserved.

45. Which of the following is NOT true about purposeful sampling?

a. It may be comprehensive with every case or instance being selected
b. The researchers intend to generalize their findings to the population
c. The researchers may select examples of only the most extreme cases
d. The researchers may select examples of only the most typical cases

46. Which of the following statements is true when considering cultural and familial influences on self-esteem?

a. Chinese and Japanese children have higher self-esteem than North American children, mainly because their cultures have higher academic standards for achievement
b. Boys tend to have lower self-esteem than girls
c. African American children tend to have lower self-esteem than Caucasian children
d. An authoritative parenting style usually allows children to have especially high self-esteem

47. The role of the therapist in strategic family therapy is all of the following EXCEPT:

a. find the myth that keeps a behavior going.
b. understand levels of communication.
c. focus on levels of organization.
d. overcome feelings of inferiority.

48. The only test a counselor is using with her client has a reliability of 0.60, so she should:

a. feel confident that the results are accurate.
b. consider the results to be questionable, but still acceptable.
c. disregard the results of the test as the reliability is too low.
d. realize that the reliability is low, but still consider the test to be acceptable.

49. In "rater bias," a supervisor who rates an employee negatively overall simply because of one very negative attribute is using what type of rater bias?

a. Halo
b. Severity
c. Horns
d. Recency

50. When counseling a client who is self-identified as a lesbian and whom the counselor believes is marginalized, which of the following should be the first step?

a. Outline the ways in which the client may be marginalized
b. Determine if the client feels marginalized
c. Guide the client to becoming more aware of being marginalized
d. Explore how marginalization has affected the client's life

51. If a group has co-leaders, which of the following is true?

a. Both co-leaders should always have the same amount of group experience
b. It is better if both co-leaders are the same sex (two males or two females)
c. Co-leaders with different theoretical orientations create a better dynamic
d. Different reactions from co-leaders can help stimulate group energy and discussions

Copyright © Mometrix Media. You have been licensed one copy of this document for personal use only. Any other reproduction or redistribution is strictly prohibited. All rights reserved.

52. What does multicultural/diversity counseling refer to?

    a. Counseling that recognizes diversity and approaches beneficial to specific groups
    b. Counseling that attempts to minimize the cultural aspects of particular groups
    c. An approach that all counselors should ethically be aware of
    d. Both A and C

53. Which is NOT included in the conditions required for a successful malpractice claim against a therapist?

    a. A professional relationship was established
    b. There was a breach of duty causing an injury
    c. The client disliked the counselor's methods
    d. A client was physically or psychically injured

54. Throughout the entire psychosocial assessment, the client maintains the same sad expression. Which of the following terms best describes the client's affect?

    a. Restricted
    b. Flat
    c. Inappropriate
    d. Blunted

55. If a mental health client is making statements that seem to be based on delusional thinking, such as "My doctor is constantly flirting with me," the best way to express doubt is by which of the following statements?

    a. "I don't believe that."
    b. "You must be kidding!"
    c. "Are you telling me the truth?"
    d. "That's hard to believe."

56. The Eskimo word "piblokto" refers to "arctic hysteria" characterized by uncontrolled screaming and crying that is often accompanied by running through the snow naked. This is an example of what kind of disorder?

    a. Culture-specific
    b. Culture shock
    c. Culture free
    d. Cross-cultural

57. According to Freud, _____ is the most important defense mechanism. An example of this defense mechanism is when a woman who has been physically abused by her spouse doesn't remember ever being hurt by him.

    a. regression
    b. repression
    c. reaction formation
    d. denial

Copyright © Mometrix Media. You have been licensed one copy of this document for personal use only. Any other reproduction or redistribution is strictly prohibited. All rights reserved.

58. An 18-year-old student wants to view his educational records. The best course of action is to:

    a. get parent permission before disclosing this information.
    b. talk him out of it.
    c. give him access to these records.
    d. ignore his request.

59. A client with schizophrenia with catatonia has sat in the same chair with the right arm extended for an hour after the phlebotomist extended the arm for a blood draw. This is an example of which of the following?

    a. Posturing
    b. Waxy flexibility
    c. Anergia
    d. Mimicry

60. Harry is a little boy whose parents have taken him to a behavior therapist. The parents want some help getting him to clean up his room, go to bed on time, get dressed for school in the morning, and complete other similar daily activities without a struggle or a big fight. The therapist makes a chart for Harry. Every time he completes a desired behavior, he gets a gold star on the chart for that activity. At the end of each week, he and his parents count his gold stars, and he gets a reward based on the number of stars—a pizza or ice cream treat, a movie, etc.—something he values. Which of the following is the most accurate name for the technique that Harry's therapist is using?

    a. Token economy
    b. Reinforcement schedule
    c. Systematic desensitization
    d. Negative reinforcement

61. In existential therapy, what do umwelt, mitwelt, and eigenwelt mean respectively?

    a. Identity of self, physical system, relationships
    b. Physical system, relationships, identity of self
    c. Relationships, identity of self, physical system
    d. Identity of self, relationships, physical system

62. Which of the following would least relate to one of Lazarus' seven modalities?

    a. The act of standing up or of sitting down
    b. A perception of an odor that doesn't exist
    c. Having a conversation with an acquaintance
    d. Having an idea about how to solve a problem

63. Which of the following is an example of feedback that is directed at an action that the client cannot modify?

    a. "Your comment is inappropriate."
    b. "You seem angry at your therapist."
    c. "You have memory problems because of your alcohol abuse."
    d. "I noticed that you didn't make eye contact with your son."

Copyright © Mometrix Media. You have been licensed one copy of this document for personal use only. Any other reproduction or redistribution is strictly prohibited. All rights reserved.

64. Multiple-choice items like those found on the NCE tap skills primarily of:

- a. organization.
- b. planning.
- c. recognition.
- d. recall.

65. An adolescent male is seeing the counselor after he was arrested along with four other boys for breaking into a school and vandalizing it as part of an initiation into a club. The client states he was aware that what he was doing was wrong but didn't question and went along with the group anyway. This is an example of which dynamic that can take place in a group?

- a. Diffusion of responsibility
- b. Deindividuation
- c. Mob action
- d. Psychopathy

66. A counselor may decide to administer a number of personality tests in order to:

- a. better understand the client.
- b. predict future performance.
- c. evaluate the outcomes of counseling.
- d. all of the above.

67. A therapy group for women who have suffered intimate partner violence has agreed to avoid making negative comments about each other, but during one discussion, one member tells another, "You are a complete idiot if you believe your husband is going to change his behavior!" Which of the following is the most appropriate response?

- a. "I can see you are concerned, but we have agreed to avoid negative comments about each other."
- b. "You are violating the rules of conduct by calling her an idiot."
- c. "You need to stop making negative comments!"
- d. "What did we agree on about the rules of conduct?"

68. A client who worries about how she looks and checks her appearance in the mirror repeatedly for 4 to 5 hours every day and has had repeated plastic surgical procedures is diagnosed with body dysmorphic disorder. The client has been prescribed an SSRI by a psychiatrist. Which approach to therapy is most indicated?

- a. Habit reversal training
- b. Psychoanalysis
- c. Cognitive restructuring
- d. Motivational interviewing

69. Robert Carkhuff proposed a five-point scale to measure the quality of a counselor's empathic responses. Which level does the following example best represent? Client: Oh, my wife yelled at me so bad you wouldn't believe it! It just killed me!!! Counselor: What did she say?

- a. Level 1
- b. Level 2
- c. Level 3
- d. Level 4-5

Copyright © Mometrix Media. You have been licensed one copy of this document for personal use only. Any other reproduction or redistribution is strictly prohibited. All rights reserved.

70. The role of the professional career counselor involves which of the following:

    a. facilitating self-awareness.
    b. teaching decision-making skills.
    c. teaching employability skills.
    d. The counselor's role involves all of the above

71. Two clients are referred to a counselor and deemed to be "workaholics." One enjoys his work, and the other does not. Which is likely to be more problematic?

    a. The client who enjoys his work
    b. The client who does not enjoy his work
    c. Neither is likely to be problematic
    d. Both are likely to be equally problematic

72. Hypnotherapy is used today for:

    a. headaches.
    b. childbirth.
    c. chronic pain.
    d. all of the above.

73. If a client has a smoking habit, Sigmund Freud might say he is:

    a. in need of behavioral therapy.
    b. anal-retentive.
    c. orally fixated.
    d. in the latent period.

74. Raymond Cattell's "factor analysis" theory refers to three types of traits. What are they?

    a. Source, surface, and unique
    b. Original, modulating, and final
    c. New, old, and resolved
    d. Complex, simple, and modulated

75. A client's employer has mandated that she take an immediate vacation. She is resistant, feeling she needs to work harder to prove herself. The company's concern, however, may more likely be related to:

    a. cost-cutting techniques.
    b. the eventual elimination of her job.
    c. occupational stress.
    d. interpersonal conflicts.

76. Paradoxical intention, implosive therapy, and thought stopping are all techniques used by _____ counselors.

    a. Psychoanalytic
    b. Behavioral
    c. TA
    d. Reality therapy

Copyright © Mometrix Media. You have been licensed one copy of this document for personal use only. Any other reproduction or redistribution is strictly prohibited. All rights reserved.

77. According to conjoint family therapy, it is important to look at patterns of communication and meta-communication. Meta-communication can be defined as those aspects of communication:

    a. involving how something is said, not what is said.
    b. involving what is said.
    c. that are hidden.
    d. that are direct and open.

78. An outpatient client with generalized anxiety disorder (GAD) has as an emotional support animal (a cat) and wants to take the cat to work with her when she returns to her job. According to Title II and Title III of the Americans with Disabilities Act, which of the following is true about an emotional comfort animal?

    a. It does not qualify as a service animal
    b. It must be accommodated by employers as a service animal
    c. It can be certified as a service animal only if it is a dog
    d. It is certified as a service animal only on special request

79. A(n) _____ schedule of reinforcement is the most difficult to extinguish.

    a. intermittent
    b. consistent
    c. systematic
    d. ratio

80. The Hamilton Rating Scale for Depression is intended for which of the following?

    a. Diagnosing depression
    b. Self-assessment of depression
    c. Determining the severity of diagnosed depression
    d. Determining suicidal ideation associated with depression

81. A client was involved in a severe accident that resulted in the death of the client's spouse and child, but in the hours since the accident, the client has been unable to recall anything about the accident. Which of the following types of amnesia is the client likely experiencing?

    a. Selective
    b. Localized
    c. Generalized
    d. Systematized

82. Under the ethical principles of informed consent, a counselor must inform each client of:

    a. the limits of confidentiality.
    b. her credentials.
    c. issues related to third-party billing and missed appointments.
    d. Both A and C.

83. Which of the following does NOT use John Holland's typology for determining a person's career type?

    a. The Vocational Preference Inventory
    b. The Self-Directed Search
    c. The Career Pattern Study
    d. The Career Assessment Inventory

Copyright © Mometrix Media. You have been licensed one copy of this document for personal use only. Any other reproduction or redistribution is strictly prohibited. All rights reserved.

84. A seventeen-year-old client has been referred for intellectual testing. What test is likely to be performed?

    a. WAIS-IV
    b. WISC-R
    c. WPPSI
    d. Rorschach

85. In psychoanalytic theory, a dream's "manifest content" is:

    a. its conscious material.
    b. its unconscious material.
    c. its interpretation.
    d. its real-life application.

86. A client has difficulty with both verbal and nonverbal communication that is appropriate for the social context, is unable to match communication to the needs of the listener, and has difficulty recognizing clues for turn-taking but exhibits no repetitive motor movements, fixated interests, or abnormal response to sensory input. These signs and symptoms are characteristic of which of the following?

    a. Autism spectrum disorder, level 1
    b. Autism spectrum disorder, level 2
    c. Autism spectrum disorder, level 3
    d. Social (pragmatic) communication disorder

87. According to the "bystander effect," an individual is ___ likely to help someone in need if that individual is the only other person present.

    a. more
    b. less
    c. just as
    d. not

88. When counseling a client with PTSD, which of the following advice should the counselor advise the client to follow?

    a. Try to avoid thinking about the traumatic experience
    b. Avoid all stressful social situations
    c. Talk about problems with support people
    d. Stay alert at all times

89. A group that is focused on a central theme such as anger management or learning job seeking skills is known as a:

    a. structured group.
    b. self-help group.
    c. psychoeducation group.
    d. T-group.

Copyright © Mometrix Media. You have been licensed one copy of this document for personal use only. Any other reproduction or redistribution is strictly prohibited. All rights reserved.

90. An 8-year-old boy has been sleeping poorly, complaining of stomachaches, crying frequently, and refusing to go to school. A complete physical examination ruled out a physical ailment. As part of an assessment for anxiety, which of the following is the simplest assessment tool to use with a child?

a. Hamilton Anxiety Scale (HAS)
b. Beck Anxiety Inventory (BAI)
c. Beck Depression Inventory (BDI)
d. Revised Children's Manifest Anxiety Scale (RCMAS)

91. Convergent validation and discriminant validation occur within what type of validity?

a. Content validity
b. Predictive validity
c. Construct validity
d. Concurrent validity

92. If a client expresses great anxiety and fears about an upcoming meeting with her employer, and the counselor asks, "What is the worst thing that can happen?", which of the following approaches is the counselor utilizing?

a. Distraction
b. Rationalization
c. Thought stopping
d. Decatastrophizing

93. Which of the following is NOT a reason to use nonparametric statistics?

a. There is a homogeneous sample
b. There is a normal score distribution
c. There are two independent samples
d. There is nominal (categorical) data

94. Reinforcement _____ the likelihood of the behavior to occur again, and punishment _____ the likelihood of the behavior to occur again.

a. increases; increases
b. decreases; increases
c. increases; decreases
d. decreases; decreases

95. What is abnormal behavior?

a. Behavior that is maladaptive and harmful
b. Behavior that is atypical
c. Behavior that is not "normal"
d. Behavior that is different from that of the individual's peer group

96. Which of the following is the best approach to minimizing or eliminating test bias?

a. Creating separate norm groups for different groups against whom the test is thought to be biased
b. Having a panel of experts review the test items before standardizing the test
c. Pre-screening examiners to be used in the standardization process for any possible prejudicial feelings
d. Screening test items for possible bias

Copyright © Mometrix Media. You have been licensed one copy of this document for personal use only. Any other reproduction or redistribution is strictly prohibited. All rights reserved.

97. The counselor is assisting with a research study in which half of the subjects are given medication and the other half given sugar pills. Neither group knows which pills contain medication, yet many who receive the sugar pills repeatedly report positive effects from taking them. What would account for this?

a. Transference
b. The placebo effect
c. The Hawthorne effect
d. Research bias

98. What's the Myers-Briggs Type Indicator?

a. A test for personality disorders
b. A personality test
c. An intelligence test
d. A test of neurological function

99. A client who is an airline pilot is facing mandatory retirement and reports feeling increasing stress and anxiety because his retirement income is considerably less than his current income and he still has young children from a second marriage. The client states he is unsure what he will do with his time and is unsure of his job skills. Which of the following adjunctive services may most benefit the client?

a. Recreational therapy
b. Vocational counseling
c. Webinars and online courses regarding retirement
d. Financial counseling

100. A client admits to the counselor that she drinks 2 to 3 large glasses of wine daily in order to relieve stress but feels this is not a concern even though she recently was involved in an automobile accident and was arrested for drunk driving. The client is likely in which stage of substance abuse?

a. Regular use
b. Problem use
c. Dependence
d. Addiction

101. Which of the following is true regarding validity and reliability of tests?

a. Validity is how consistent the test is
b. A test may be reliable, but not valid
c. A test may be valid, but not reliable
d. Reliability is specific to the situation

102. Changes in human growth and development that are qualitative are:

a. changes in number, degree, or frequency.
b. changes in structure or organization.
c. changes which are sequential.
d. changes which are discontinuous.

Copyright © Mometrix Media. You have been licensed one copy of this document for personal use only. Any other reproduction or redistribution is strictly prohibited. All rights reserved.

103. The Minnesota Importance Questionnaire can be used with:

   a. males only.
   b. males or females.
   c. groups only.
   d. individuals only.

104. Albert Bandura's best-known research was his:

   a. psychoanalytic attachment study.
   b. Little Albert experiment.
   c. Bobo doll study.
   d. behavioral contrast research.

105. Down syndrome is caused by:

   a. prenatal drug use.
   b. environmental factors.
   c. poor parenting.
   d. a chromosomal abnormality.

106. Which group of students would be least likely to seek out career counseling?

   a. Students in high school or middle school
   b. Students with high responsibilities at home such as taking care of younger siblings.
   c. Students entering college
   d. Students who were taking college prep courses in high school

107. A client who recently learned he had kidney cancer has been researching everything he can about the disease, treatment, and outlook. Which defense mechanism is the client utilizing?

   a. Rationalization
   b. Repression
   c. Intellectualism
   d. Compensation

108. A 22-year-old female is receiving haloperidol for schizoaffective disorder. She was admitted to the psychiatric unit with delusional thinking, rapid disorganized speech, irritability, and lethargy. She has begun slapping at his face repeatedly. Which assessment tool is most indicated?

   a. Abnormal Involuntary Movement Scale (AIMS)
   b. CAGE
   c. Minim-mental state exam (MMSE)
   d. Confusion Assessment Method

109. In a group therapy setting, what is a "gate keeper"?

   a. A way to ensure that therapy goals are set and consistently met
   b. The individual who ensures the group remains "open" or "closed"
   c. A role assumed by a group therapy member
   d. The means by which therapy goals are safeguarded

Copyright © Mometrix Media. You have been licensed one copy of this document for personal use only. Any other reproduction or redistribution is strictly prohibited. All rights reserved.

110. A client with a long history of alcoholism had worked as an engineer but has been unemployed for four years and is now in early stages of recovery and wants to find work. The counselor should advise the client to do which of the following?

    a. Apply for engineering jobs
    b. Wait to apply for work for at least 6 months
    c. Contact previous employers about jobs
    d. Apply for jobs that are less demanding

111. Someone who always agrees with anything the other group therapy members say is:

    a. nonassertive.
    b. assertive.
    c. passive aggressive.
    d. play-acting.

112. When one member of a group begins to exhibit negative nonverbal communication (such as eye-rolling or looking bored), the counselor, who is serving as the group leader, routinely directs the group's attention toward another member of the group by asking the other group member a question or making a comment. Which of the following does this best exemplify?

    a. Linking
    b. Blocking
    c. Facilitating
    d. Delegating

113. Altruism may be explained by:

    a. the leadership contingency model.
    b. the social exchange theory.
    c. catharsis.
    d. matching hypothesis.

114. The counselor is working with a client who has just been admitted to a rehabilitation facility for treatment of alcohol addiction. Within how many hours is the client likely to begin exhibiting signs of withdrawal?

    a. 8 hours
    b. 24 hours
    c. 48 hours
    d. 96 hours

115. A client whose son has been arrested twice for drug use states that her son was forced to use drugs by other people and has no drug problem is probably utilizing which of the following ego defense mechanisms?

    a. Displacement
    b. Intellectualism
    c. Denial
    d. Rationalization

Copyright © Mometrix Media. You have been licensed one copy of this document for personal use only. Any other reproduction or redistribution is strictly prohibited. All rights reserved.

116. The first professional counseling association (and its founding year) was:
 a. the National Vocational Guidance Association in 1913.
 b. the Vocation Bureau in Boston in 1908.
 c. the American Personnel and Guidance Association in 1951.
 d. the Office of Vocational Rehabilitation in 1954.

117. What is the Minnesota Job Description Questionnaire used for?
 a. Determining what job is best for the client specific to Minnesota
 b. Describing the characteristics of jobs currently available
 c. Measuring the reinforcing characteristics of an occupation
 d. A survey to evaluate job satisfaction

118. Which of the following is a warning sign that a counselor is developing a relationship with a client that is too personal?
 a. Enjoying meeting with the client
 b. Recognizing that the client's values are different from the counselor's values
 c. Feeling attracted to a client but not acting on the attraction
 d. Asking the client about personal matters unrelated to client's needs

119. Ann Roe believed that all EXCEPT which of these elements influence occupational selection?
 a. Genetic factors
 b. Environmental influences
 c. Parent-child relationships
 d. Cognitive development

120. Who theorized about "primary narcissism"?
 a. Jung
 b. Freud
 c. Adler
 d. Rogers

121. A parent stops the counselor and asks, "Could you tell me what is wrong with the client across the hall from my son? He seems so agitated." Which of the following responses complies with the Health Insurance Portability and Accountability Act (HIPAA)?
 a. "The law doesn't allow me to give out any information about clients in order to protect their privacy and safety."
 b. "His mother is in the lounge. You can go ask her."
 c. "Why are you asking?"
 d. "He has bipolar disease, like your son."

122. Which of these is NOT generally identified as a circumstance in which testing may be useful?
 a. Job or educational placement
 b. Counseling
 c. Diagnosis
 d. None of these

Copyright © Mometrix Media. You have been licensed one copy of this document for personal use only. Any other reproduction or redistribution is strictly prohibited. All rights reserved.

123. In contrast to a homogeneous group, a heterogeneous group:

a. is more cohesive and supportive.
b. has members with greater awareness of themselves and others.
c. has less conflict among participants.
d. focuses on one specific problem.

124. Which of the following is NOT an advantage of group counseling?

a. Cost-effectiveness
b. Focus on individual needs
c. Opportunities for feedback
d. Structured practice

125. Would Freud's psychodynamic approach and Albert Ellis' REBT favor the emic or the etic approach?

a. They would both favor the etic approach
b. They would both favor the emic approach
c. Freud would favor the etic approach and Ellis the emic
d. Freud would favor the emic approach and Ellis the etic

126. Which of the following are four core elements in building a helping relationship?

a. Friendship, knowledge, cultural foundations, direction
b. Leadership, skills, empathy, emotional influence
c. Human relations, social influence, skills, theory
d. Assertiveness, social influence, knowledge, theory

127. A 42-year-old woman returns to her career as an HR manager after her children start to attend school all day. This is an example of:

a. a re-entry woman.
b. a displaced homemaker.
c. gender bias.
d. wage discrimination.

128. The goals of what type of therapy include gaining knowledge about the self and recognizing and integrating the self?

a. Adlerian
b. Jungian
c. Existential
d. Freudian

129. What are some common criticisms of Rogerian therapy?

a. It doesn't take developmental stages into account
b. It assumes that people are basically good and healthy
c. It may be inappropriate for some type of mental illness
d. All of the above

81

Copyright © Mometrix Media. You have been licensed one copy of this document for personal use only. Any other reproduction or redistribution is strictly prohibited. All rights reserved.

130. Which of these books was authored by Eric Berne?

    a. I'm OK – You're OK
    b. In And Out of the Garbage Can
    c. Games People Play
    d. On Becoming a Person

131. One family structure that is on the rise in the United States is the:

    a. blended family.
    b. multigenerational family.
    c. single-parent family.
    d. homosexual family.

132. Believing that the significant other of an individual must love them for anything they do, would be an example from what theory?

    a. REBT
    b. Psychoanalytic theory
    c. Aversive therapy
    d. Operant conditioning

133. The psychodynamic model has a _____ unit of study; the experiential model has a _____ unit of study; the transgenerational model has a _____ unit of study; and the strategic model has a _____ unit of study.

    a. monadic; dyadic; triadic; dyadic and triadic
    b. dyadic; monadic; monadic and dyadic; triadic
    c. monadic; dyadic and triadic; triadic; dyadic
    d. triadic; monadic and dyadic; dyadic; triadic

134. What is J. P. Guilford known for?

    a. Developing IQ testing for mental patients
    b. Studying inherited intellectual qualities
    c. Investigating individual differences and intellect
    d. Intellectual testing of children with autism

135. If a client is taking Thorazine, he's taking an:

    a. Antidepressant
    b. Antipsychotic
    c. Antidepressant
    d. Antispasmodic

136. If using functional family therapy (FFT) to work with the family of a 17-year-old client with antisocial behavior and a history of escalating delinquency, which of the following is the first phase?

    a. Generalization
    b. Engagement/motivation
    c. Behavior change
    d. Awareness

Copyright © Mometrix Media. You have been licensed one copy of this document for personal use only. Any other reproduction or redistribution is strictly prohibited. All rights reserved.

137. Career choices as expressions of one's personality are to _____ as career choices as influenced by genetic endowment, environmental factors, and previous learning experiences are to _____.

   a. Krumboltz; Holland
   b. Holland; Krumboltz
   c. Roe; Krumboltz
   d. Holland; Roe

138. Four broad stages of development in the first three years of life are identified in object relations theory. Which of these represents the correct chronological order of these four stages?

   a. Fusion with mother; Symbiosis with mother; Separation/individuation; Constancy of self and object
   b. Symbiosis with mother; Fusion with mother; Separation/individuation; Constancy of self and object
   c. Constancy of self and object; Separation/individuation; Symbiosis with mother; Fusion with mother
   d. Separation/individuation; Constancy of self and object; Symbiosis with mother; Fusion with mother

139. _____ is a disorder of thought, unlike _____, which is a disorder of mood.

   a. Borderline; conduct disorder
   b. Conduct disorder; depression
   c. Bipolar disorder; schizophrenia
   d. Schizophrenia; bipolar disorder

140. A client with court-ordered therapy for antisocial personality disorder is very manipulative and exhibits unacceptable behavior. Part of his therapy includes limit setting. If the client asks the counselor a personal question, such as "Do you live with your boyfriend?" which of the following is the most appropriate response?

   a. "That is none of your business."
   b. "It is not appropriate to ask me personal questions."
   c. "Why are you asking me that?"
   d. "What is the rule about these types of questions?"

141. MMPI-A and CPI are to _____ as Rorschach and TAT are to _____.

   a. interest inventories; subjective tests.
   b. objective tests; interest inventories.
   c. objective tests; standardized tests.
   d. objective tests; subjective tests.

142. What would Erich Fromm have said about religion?

   a. It may inhibit healthy growth and development
   b. It may be used to encourage warfare
   c. It's fine to have religious faith and experience
   d. All of the above

Copyright © Mometrix Media. You have been licensed one copy of this document for personal use only. Any other reproduction or redistribution is strictly prohibited. All rights reserved.

143. A counselor is focusing on social skills training with a client with schizophrenia in order to improve the client's ability to function socially. The counselor is utilizing shaping to reinforce teaching. Which of the following is the best description of shaping?

  a. Rewarding improvement steps toward the target behavior goal
  b. Repeating the same teaching over and over again
  c. Asking the client to describe the emotional response to each lesson
  d. Using illustrations and videos to demonstrate target behaviors

144. When beginning a counseling relationship, the counselor is ethically required to:

  a. inform the patient of the limits of confidentiality.
  b. explain that everything said during sessions will remain confidential.
  c. keep a detailed record of what is said during each session.
  d. write very few details of what is said during each session.

145. What is a "token economy"?

  a. A behavioral modification technique
  b. A temporary, experimental economic system
  c. A way to test a societal economic construct
  d. A new type of dream analysis

146. Susie is playing with blocks and is trying to build a tower; she tries but cannot build a tower. Susie's mother helps her build a four-block tower. Later, Susie builds a four-block tower without her mother's help. According to Vygotsky, the inability to build the tower on her own is known as:

  a. scaffolding.
  b. the zone of proximal development.
  c. assisted discovery.
  d. learning by imitation.

147. A counselor is court-ordered to disclose confidential information about a client he is counseling. What does the counselor do?

  a. Limit, as much as possible, any possibly damaging personal information
  b. Divulge any and all information about the client as court-ordered
  c. Obtain written permission from the client to share confidential information
  d. Both A and C

148. If a 27-year-old client with narcissistic personality disorder is pregnant and has made plans to have an abortion but the counselor is opposed to abortion for religious reasons, the counselor should do which of the following?

  a. Discuss alternatives with the client
  b. Provide literature about adoption
  c. Advise the client her decision is morally wrong
  d. Support the client's decision

Copyright © Mometrix Media. You have been licensed one copy of this document for personal use only. Any other reproduction or redistribution is strictly prohibited. All rights reserved.

149. There are many confounding variables that can threaten an experiment's validity, but which of the following is a threat to both internal validity and external validity?

a. Attrition (mortality)
b. Instrumentation
c. Selection of subjects
d. Experimenter bias

150. The evidence-based Suicide Assessment Five-step Evaluation and Triage (SAFE-T) tool indicates that a client has modifiable risk factors for suicide and strong protective factors, resulting in an overall low risk factor although the client admits to thoughts of death but denies a plan or intent. Which of the following is the intervention that is most indicated?

a. Outpatient treatment and crisis numbers
b. Crisis plan and crisis numbers
c. Admission to inpatient facility and crisis plan
d. Admission to inpatient facility with suicide precautions

151. What does a "correlation strategy" measure?

a. How strong the relation is between things
b. The way in which the experiment is conducted
c. The "strategy" for graphing the experiment's results
d. The validity of a research study

152. A "V" code in the DSM is the:

a. clinical syndrome.
b. focus of treatment that is not attributable to a specific mental condition.
c. code used when personality disorders are present.
d. global assessment of function.

153. A career counselor is interested in keeping up with trends in the job market so that they can better assist their clients. One of the best ways to keep up with the trends in the job market is to consult the:

a. OOH.
b. DOT.
c. Wall Street Journal.
d. SOC.

154. If a counselor is conducting an experiment and chooses a significance level of .01, what does this mean?

a. It means that the counselor is willing to accept the possibility of erring in accepting or rejecting the null hypothesis one time out of one hundred
b. It means that the counselor is willing to accept the possibility of erring in conducting the experiment in one percent of the trials made
c. It means that the counselor is willing to accept the possibility that the instruments will err in their measurements one out of ten times
d. It means that the counselor is willing to accept the possibility that the hypothesis will be wrong in ten out of one hundred experiments

Copyright © Mometrix Media. You have been licensed one copy of this document for personal use only. Any other reproduction or redistribution is strictly prohibited. All rights reserved.

155. A young woman comes into the office complaining of loss of appetite, nervousness (even when in a safe, relaxed setting), and recurrent nightmares of a past hospital experience from years prior, where she says she almost died. What might the counselor suspect?

a. Substance abuse
b. Panic disorder
c. Schizophrenia
d. PTSD

156. A survey researcher has asked Larry and Carol about their attitudes toward obeying laws. They are asked what they would do in certain hypothetical situations. For example, if the only way to help someone and/or to avoid harming someone would involve breaking the law. "Law, schmaw, what's important is doing the right thing," said Carol. "True, we should do what's right, but we've also made an agreement with society to follow its rules. We should try to do that too, but I agree that a lot of it depends on the situation," said Larry. How did Larry and Carol fit in Kohlberg's stages of moral development?

a. Larry is in Stage 1 and Carol is in Stage 2
b. Larry is in Stage 4 and Carol is in Stage 3
c. Larry is in Stage 5 and Carol is in Stage 6
d. Larry is in Stage 4 and Carol is in Stage 5

157. Which one of the following does NOT belong with the other three?

a. Horney
b. Glasser
c. Adler
d. Jung

158. The counselor is concerned about how her group therapy sessions are progressing. What can she do?

a. Have an outside observer assess the group
b. She can evaluate the group dynamics herself
c. Ask her group members to each evaluate the group sessions
d. Choose a single group member to evaluate the group dynamics

159. Children who are diagnosed with conduct disorder at a young age (preteen) are most at risk for which of the following personality disorders as adults?

a. Borderline personality disorder
b. Histrionic personality disorder
c. Antisocial personality disorder
d. Narcissistic personality disorder

Copyright © Mometrix Media. You have been licensed one copy of this document for personal use only. Any other reproduction or redistribution is strictly prohibited. All rights reserved.

160. Christine's new therapist believes that clients' problems have social and political sources, and that one's personal and social identities are interconnected. The therapist also believes that the therapeutic relationship is a collaborative process between equals, and that androcentric norms are to be rejected. To what type of theory does Christine's therapist likely adhere?

   a. Solution-focused brief therapy
   b. Narrative therapy
   c. Feminist therapy
   d. Reality therapy

161. Which of these is NOT a condition for which testing should be used?

   a. Gaining self-understanding
   b. Licensure and certification
   c. Labeling some individuals
   d. For educational planning

162. What idea is Francis Galton known for?

   a. Statistical relevance studies
   b. Inherited intellectual abilities
   c. Statistical validity studies
   d. Personality testing

163. According to Albert Bandura, observational learning happens primarily through:

   a. reinforcement.
   b. trial and error.
   c. cognition.
   d. conditioning.

164. Adlerian family therapy involves all of the following EXCEPT:

   a. overcoming feelings of inferiority.
   b. promoting social interest.
   c. pinpointing irrational beliefs.
   d. investigating goals of behavior.

165. A test producing the same results from one time to another is to a test measuring what it is supposed to as _____ is to _____.

   a. validity; reliability.
   b. reliability; validity.
   c. reliability; standardization.
   d. standardization; reliability.

166. A client with borderline personality disorder was sexually abused by her father as a child and vacillates between insisting he is a kind and loving father and a horrible abusive monster. This is an example of which of the following?

   a. Dissociative symptoms
   b. Magical thinking
   c. Rationalization
   d. Splitting

Copyright © Mometrix Media. You have been licensed one copy of this document for personal use only. Any other reproduction or redistribution is strictly prohibited. All rights reserved.

167. A client is in the maintenance stage of recovery from addiction. How long does the counselor anticipate that the maintenance stage may persist?

    a. 1 year
    b. 2 years
    c. 3 years
    d. 5 years

168. Which is one of Glasser's five fundamental needs from Choice Theory?

    a. Freedom
    b. Wealth
    c. Happiness
    d. Meaningful work

169. A 34-year-old male client who returned from miliary service in Afghanistan has begun to have severe frightening flashbacks related to post-traumatic stress syndrome (PTSD). If the counselor finds the client cowering in the corner of the room in a state of panic, the best approach is to say which of the following?

    a. "Give me your hand and I'll help you up."
    b. "I know you are afraid, but you are safe here."
    c. "Just breathe deeply and relax."
    d. "There is nothing to be afraid of."

170. Connie tells each of her clients that the best way she can help them is to attempt to look at the world from the client's point of view. This counselor is taking the:

    a. etic perspective.
    b. alloplastic perspective.
    c. emic perspective.
    d. autoplastic perspective.

171. Daniel Levinson's work has been criticized as being too limited because:

    a. his developmental life stages did not include any transitional periods.
    b. he only studied the structure of life for males and excluded females.
    c. he believed that there is a midlife crisis, but many do not see a crisis.
    d. he stated that people question their lives but did not include careers.

172. In what ways do stereotypes distort reality?

    a. Stereotypes exaggerate the differences that exist between groups
    b. Stereotypes exaggerate the differences that exist within groups
    c. Stereotypes produce many differing perceptions by many people
    d. Stereotypes demonstrate that members of a group can be different

173. Developed by Luft and Ingham, _____ asserts that there are four parts to the personality: the public self, the blind self, the private self, and the unknown self.

    a. neurolinguistic programming
    b. the concept of the collective unconscious
    c. the concept of the family constellation
    d. the concept of the Johari window

Copyright © Mometrix Media. You have been licensed one copy of this document for personal use only. Any other reproduction or redistribution is strictly prohibited. All rights reserved.

174. Which of these is a LESS appropriate rationale for a counselor's use of testing?
a. To help predict a client's future performance in school, work, or training
b. To critique the client's performance in a school, work or training setting
c. To help clients to make decisions regarding their school or work futures
d. To help clients to identify interests they may not have known they had

175. Which of the following is the most accurate statement regarding integrative counseling?
a. Integrative counseling the same type of counseling as eclectic counseling
b. Integrative counseling begins with techniques and ends with the therapist's personal theory
c. Integrative counseling is a highly generalized theory that makes much use of incongruence
d. Integrative counseling synthesizes processes and techniques from various theoretical views

176. What would G. L. Harrington or William Glasser most likely say regarding transference?
a. It is a normal process in therapy that can be analyzed and resolved
b. It impedes progress and need not occur if the therapist is genuine
c. It is disregarded as an internal state without observable behaviors
d. It is encouraged, and it is used as an exploratory therapeutic tool

177. There are various stages in group therapy. Which of the following is one of them?
a. Sublimation
b. Invitation
c. Initiation
d. Storming

178. A counselor has written a book and an accompanying workbook on managing panic. The counselor requires each of her clients who is being seen for a panic disorder to purchase these materials. This is:
a. ethical, since these are treatment materials.
b. not unethical but unacceptable.
c. financially feasible for the clients.
d. unethical.

179. A client believes that messages are being sent to her in newspapers, magazines, radio, and television and that she must decipher them. This type of delusion is classified as which of the following?
a. Delusion of persecution
b. Delusion of control
c. Delusion of reference
d. Delusion of grandeur

180. A client nearing the end-of-life because of a terminal disease tells the counselor that she feels that her life was wasted. Which of the following may be most beneficial?
a. Reassuring the client
b. Guiding the client to carry out a life review
c. Advising the client to make peace with her life choices
d. Encouraging the client to exercise more control over end-of-life issues

Copyright © Mometrix Media. You have been licensed one copy of this document for personal use only. Any other reproduction or redistribution is strictly prohibited. All rights reserved.

181. A cultural norm refers to:

    a. how people are supposed to act.

    b. how people act.

    c. how people would ideally like to act.

    d. all of the above.

182. When counseling young children in a group setting, it is helpful to enlist the involvement of:

    a. parents.

    b. siblings.

    c. teachers.

    d. pastoral professionals.

183. A man has been arrested for a crime. His former counselor is called to perform a forensic evaluation. What is the counselor's responsibility in this case?

    a. It is not considered ethical to perform a forensic evaluation on a current or past client, so the counselor should decline

    b. The counselor should perform the evaluation because they are particularly well-versed on the mental state of the individual in question

    c. The counselor has a legal responsibility to comply with the request

    d. It doesn't matter if the counselor performs the evaluation or not

184. A 32-year-old woman with borderline personality disorder and history of attempted suicide has been married for 8 years, but her husband is filing for divorce. She was found wandering in a state of confused panic about her neighborhood and brought to the ED. She feels extremely anxious and abandoned. Which initial intervention is appropriate for this emotional crisis?

    a. Stay with the client and reassure her

    b. Administer anti-anxiety medication

    c. Provide positive reinforcement

    d. Draw up a no-suicide contract

185. If a client with substance abuse disorder states he has been using "beanies," the counselor should understand that the client is referring to which of the following?

    a. Marijuana

    b. Cocaine

    c. Methamphetamine

    d. Heroin

186. A client has been diagnosed with narcissistic personality disorder. Which of the following is generally the recommended therapeutic approach?

    a. Cognitive behavioral therapy

    b. Mindfulness-based therapy

    c. Group therapy

    d. Psychotherapy (talk therapy)

Copyright © Mometrix Media. You have been licensed one copy of this document for personal use only. Any other reproduction or redistribution is strictly prohibited. All rights reserved.

187. Which of the following may the counselor recommend as interventions for a client that is having hallucinations?

a. Reality-based activities
b. Meditation and relaxation exercises
c. Psychoeducation
d. Cognitive restructuring

188. Which of the following is NOT an intelligence test?

a. WISC-V
b. WAIS-IV
c. MMPI-II
d. WPPSI-IV

189. A marriage and family counselor treating a 10-year-old daughter and her mother tells the daughter that if she loads the dishwasher on Mondays, Wednesdays, and Fridays, then she and her mother will go shopping at the mall on Saturday. The counselor then has the mother and the daughter sign a contract to that effect. This is an example of:

a. the Premack principle.
b. negative reinforcement.
c. shaping through successive approximations.
d. quid pro quo.

190. A client, from a family of six children, is extremely conservative and responsible but suffers from feelings of inferiority. According to Alfred Adler's birth-order theory, which place in the family is this client likely to reside?

a. Last born
b. First born
c. Third born
d. Fifth born

191. If a client states, "I don't understand! My daughter said that she had to leave town," which of the following is an appropriate clarifying response?

a. "Your daughter said she had to leave town?"
b. "Are you confused because you don't know why she had to leave town?"
c. "Did she say anything else about it?"
d. "Why don't you call her and ask for more information?"

192. Emotion-focused coping is:

a. usually the best coping strategy.
b. less effective overall than problem-focused coping.
c. rarely a good coping strategy.
d. more effective overall than problem-focused coping.

Copyright © Mometrix Media. You have been licensed one copy of this document for personal use only. Any other reproduction or redistribution is strictly prohibited. All rights reserved.

193. When assessing a 35-year-old Arab American female, the counselor notes that, while discussing her family, the client uses a louder voice than while discussing other issues. This probably means that issues about her family are which of the following?

    a. A private matter
    b. A cause for shame
    c. Of lesser importance than other issues
    d. Of special importance

194. A 60-year-old client in a stable long-term relationship comes to see the counselor because he has begun to experience erectile dysfunction. Which of the following should the counselor consider initially?

    a. Referral to a urologist
    b. Couple's therapy
    c. Psychodynamic therapy
    d. Cognitive behavioral therapy

195. A client has been out of the workforce for ten years while caring for small children. She would generally be considered a:

    a. good candidate for employment.
    b. displaced homemaker.
    c. versatile employee.
    d. stay at home mother.

196. Acculturation takes place when:

    a. two cultures mix.
    b. a culture dies out.
    c. when individuals seek to deny their culture.
    d. both B and C.

197. The withdrawal of reinforcement until the conditioned response no longer occurs is known as:

    a. extinction.
    b. elimination.
    c. discrimination.
    d. punishment.

198. A high standard of counseling practice when working with diverse populations involves all of the following EXCEPT:

    a. treating all clients the same way.
    b. acknowledging and confronting their own biases and prejudices.
    c. adapting one's knowledge and skills to meet the clients' needs.
    d. educating oneself as completely as possible regarding the clients' cultural context.

Copyright © Mometrix Media. You have been licensed one copy of this document for personal use only. Any other reproduction or redistribution is strictly prohibited. All rights reserved.

199. A client wants to enter into treatment with a counselor but does not have insurance. He reports that he can afford to pay only $25 per session. The usual fee is $100. In this case, the counselor would:

    a.   refuse to see him unless he can pay the usual fee.
    b.   charge him the usual fee and have him make installment payments.
    c.   consider his financial situation and negotiate a reduced fee if this is warranted.
    d.   make a referral to someone else.

200. What type of test is the National Counselor Examination (NCE)?

    a.   Objective
    b.   Projective
    c.   Subjective
    d.   Retrospective

Copyright © Mometrix Media. You have been licensed one copy of this document for personal use only. Any other reproduction or redistribution is strictly prohibited. All rights reserved.

Answer Key and Explanations for Test #2

1. A: The Wechsler IQ test is a general test of cognitive ability. David Wechsler developed his first intelligence test, the Wechsler-Bellevue test, in 1939. That was replaced in 1955 by the Wechsler Adult Intelligence Scale (WAIS). In 1981 it was revised and called the WAIS-R. Additional updates took place in 1997, called the WAIS-III, and most recently in 2008, the current WAIS-IV. The test has eleven different subtests, and versions specific to country. The test result includes a "verbal IQ" score, a "performance IQ" score, and a "full scale IQ" score to give a well-rounded view of the individual's intellectual level and abilities.

2. A: Carl Jung believed that one's personality is not merely a product of the past, but also shaped by the present and future. He viewed personality as something that evolves over time. Jung theorized that an individual's behavior must be analyzed with its teleology (goals) in mind. He saw teleology as a process external to humans as well as a method for inquiry. For this reason, he diverted from Freud's focus on the past and its effects on the personality to theorize that all behavior will be understood by a combination of past, one's attempt to grow, and future orientation, rather than the past alone.

3. A: There are four levels of measurement. The most basic level is the nominal scale. There are no numerical values assigned, but nominal data fit into categories such as gender, numbers on a basketball jersey, or country of origin. Ordinal scale data involve rankings or order of people or objects based on a particular attribute. The numbers assigned for an ordinal scale have meaning only within the particular group. Interval scale data are calculated with the assumption that each number represents a point that is an equal distance from the point adjacent to it. Temperature is an example of an interval scale datum. Ratio scale data have an absolute zero. Weight is an example of a ratio scale datum.

4. B: Confidentiality is an ethical concept, derived from the need for an expectation of privacy in order to have a successful working relationship (i.e., little positive work can be achieved if the client fears to reveal crucial information based upon fears the information may be divulged elsewhere). By contrast, privileged communication is a legal concept, as it is granted in specific circumstances by state law – for counselors, it is often found in state licensure laws. Answer A is the reverse of the correct answer. Answers C and D are incorrect because the two concepts are not the same, and they are not both legal (C) or both ethical (D) concepts.

5. D: Negative symptoms associated with schizophrenia include blunt or flat affect, lack of energy and passivity (anergia), lack of motivation and inability to initiate tasks (avolition), poverty of speech content and speech production, and sudden interruption in speech and thought patterns so that the client may stop speaking in the middle of an idea when the client loses track of what he or she was saying (thought stopping). Negative symptoms impair social functioning and the ability to hold a job because of the client's difficulty with decision-making and communication.

6. D: A professional and ethical counselor should be alert to any and all changes in their mental status. The counselor should be able to detect when changes in their physical, psychological, and/or emotional state may be negatively affecting the ability to competently provide counseling to clients. The counselor should also be ready and willing to take the necessary measures to remove themselves from counseling should there be the need. They should also be alert to changes in colleagues and willing to assist them with their own impairments, which may affect their counseling ability.

94

Copyright © Mometrix Media. You have been licensed one copy of this document for personal use only. Any other reproduction or redistribution is strictly prohibited. All rights reserved.

7. B: R.K. Conyne felt that the understanding of the range of group experiences found in group therapy was lacking, and the Group Work Grid is a result of that concern. The Group Work Grid is composed of two dimensions. One level addresses the level of the group intervention work, and the other refers to the purpose of the group work. "Purpose" is further divided into correction and enhancement subcategories, while the level of the group work is further composed of individual, organizational, interpersonal, and community. The Group Work Grid provides a working model of group typology that has depth and practical application for the clinician.

8. C: As of the 21st century, the number of certified and licensed counselors in the United States is approaching 100,000.

9. A: Laws have changed in only some states to require insurance companies to reimburse licensed counselors, but often for only certain mental illnesses. Newer laws do NOT exist in all states of the U.S. In the states where they do exist, they do NOT cover all mental illnesses.

10. D: There is no "multiplicative" characterization of counselor responses in Carkhuff's theory. Additive refers to a response that adds noticeably (Level 4) or significantly (Level 5) to the client's affect. Subtractive refers to a response that does not attend to or detract significantly (Level 1) from the client's affect, or one that subtracts noticeably (Level 2) from the client's affect. Interchangeable refers to a response that is interchangeable (Level 3) with the client's affect.

11. C: A test with a structured procedure for administration and a specified scoring system is a better example of a standardized test. A checklist, a rating scale, or an open-ended interview are all good examples of non-standardized tests as they have no formalized or routinized directions for administering or scoring them.

12. B: An investigative type prefers systematic, intellectual activities and has poor social skills. Examples include a computer programmer or a chemist. This is Jason's predominant type. A social type dislikes activities with tools or machines and prefers activities that inform or develop other people. This is Sallie's predominant type. A realistic type is aggressive, prefers explicit activities involving physical work and has poor social skills (examples could include a mechanic or a technician). An artistic type is imaginative, prefers self-expression, and dislikes systematic and ordered activities (examples could include an artist or an editor). A conventional type is practical, prefers structured activities, and dislikes ambiguous or unsystematic work (examples could include a file clerk or an accountant). An enterprising type is an extrovert who likes leadership roles and persuasive endeavors and dislikes abstract tasks or activities requiring caution. Enterprising types might be salespersons, entrepreneurs, or those in management roles.

13. A: Interpersonal therapy is generally most effective for depressive episodes associated with specific situations (such as grief) and is usually of short duration (six 20-minute sessions). During therapy, the focus is on one issue, such as conflicts, changing roles, or grief. The client is helped to develop specific goals, and the therapist confronts the client when the client's behavior does not facilitate reaching these goals. Clients are encouraged to remain focused on the problem and to associate concrete feelings rather than abstract feelings.

14. A: Research shows that individuals who prematurely leave a group are less intelligent, poorly motivated, and high in denial. They have difficulties trusting others. Individuals who continue through the course of group counseling are open to new experiences, trusting, willing to listen to others, and empathetic. Trust is the most important characteristic for individuals who participate in group counseling. If a person is trusting, he will be more willing to open up to others, share experiences, benefit from feedback, and empathize with others. People with more limited

95

Copyright © Mometrix Media. You have been licensed one copy of this document for personal use only. Any other reproduction or redistribution is strictly prohibited. All rights reserved.

intelligence may not be able to maneuver social situations at an appropriate level of sophistication that is necessary for group success.

15. B: A factorial analysis of variance is used to determine not only significant differences between mean scores on two or more variables, but also significant interactions of the factors with each other. A one-way ANOVA determines significant difference but not significant interaction. A multivariate analysis of variance involves more than one dependent variable, but since this researcher was only measuring self-efficacy, he does not need to use it. An analysis of covariance is used when one or more independent variables are controlled with respect to their influence on the dependent variable. This research does not require such controls.

16. B: Effective is NOT a term used to describe a group leader style. (It is, however, a term used in Virginia Satir's A-B-C-D-E family therapy model to describe a healthy way of interacting.) Group leadership styles are described as autocratic or authoritarian, democratic, or laissez faire. The autocratic style may not be liked by group members, but is best for making quick decisions. The democratic style may be liked better by group, but is not always the most productive. With a cohesive, committed group, the laissez faire style often gets superior results.

17. A: Typical symptoms of schizophrenia include: grossly disorganized or catatonic behavior and/or speech, delusions and/or hallucinations, blunted affect (poor or inappropriate expressive responses to external stimuli), autism (intense self-preoccupation). Continuous signs of symptoms must be present (allowing for waxing and waning fluctuations) for six or more months. There are five types: 1) paranoid; 2) disorganized; 3) catatonic; 4) undifferentiated; and, 5) residual. Early mild symptoms are sometimes referred to as prodromal schizophrenia.

18. C: Piaget proposed that there are four stages of cognitive development. The first stage is the sensorimotor stage, whereby the infant or toddler recognizes that even though something is out of sight, it still exists (object permanence). Piaget's second stage of cognitive development is the preoperational stage (early childhood years) in which children begin to recognize that something can be an object as well as a symbol (dual representation). The third stage of cognitive development according to Piaget is called the concrete operational stage, during which children 6 to 11 years old develop the capacity of both conservation (object permanence, or the understanding that physical characteristics of objects remain the same even if the appearance is different) and reversibility (the ability to think through a series of steps and then to reverse the process mentally).

19. C: The coefficient of determination is true variance. It is obtained by squaring the correlation coefficient. In order to find the coefficient of non-determination, subtract the coefficient of determination from 1.00.

20. B: A scatter plot (or scattergram) is a type of graph that depicts pairs of scores. The x-axis of the graph shows one variable and the y-axis records the other. Each dot that is "scattered" around on the graph depicts a pair of scores collected in the experiment. The scatterplot makes it easy to see a pattern among the scores, but generally limits one to a broad generalization about the data. The scatter plot is valued in research because one can instantly see a positive or negative relationship between the data, and if that relationship is strong or weak. One can also easily see if the relationship is a linear one.

21. A: An appropriate primary intervention for clients at risk of emotional illness resulting from trauma, such as an act of violence, is to clarify the client's problem to ensure that both the client and the counselor are perceiving the problem in the same manner. Other primary interventions related to trauma include focusing on a reality approach, avoiding lengthy explanations of the problem,

Copyright © Mometrix Media. You have been licensed one copy of this document for personal use only. Any other reproduction or redistribution is strictly prohibited. All rights reserved.

helping the client understand what precipitated the problem, acknowledging the client's feelings, and showing unconditional acceptance.

22. B: It is not necessary that a counselor refer a client from another culture to another counselor. What is important is that the counselor demonstrates sensitivity to the needs of that client and has some knowledge about other cultures. If the cultural differences are accompanied by language differences, respectful care would include an interpreter to ensure that the patient's needs are being clearly explained and the counselor's recommendations are provided to the patient with equal clarity.

23. B: William Glasser's reality therapy emphasizes that we determine our fate and are in charge of our lives. Rollo May's existential therapy says we have freedom of choice and are responsible for our fate. B. F. Skinner became the primary proponent of behaviorism, which is deterministic and mechanistic in nature. Arnold Lazarus created multimodal therapy, which is holistic and eclectic in its approach but also has strong behavioral influences. These both emphasize learning rather than freedom and responsibility. Carl Rogers had a humanistic and holistic approach. While he believed the individual is self-directed, he emphasized warmth, empathy, self-acceptance and self-exploration more than personal responsibility. Heinz Kohut was a proponent of neo-Freudian psychoanalysis wherein the counselor is directive and in charge. He followed Freud's belief in unconscious motivations and biological determinism, not freedom of choice. Albert Ellis focused more on rational self-analysis than on issues of freedom or responsibility, and Eric Berne viewed the counselor as a teacher who contracts with the client for positive change. He focused on analysis of transactions and on transformations.

24. B: Because Jennifer doesn't like either of the choices, this would be an avoidance-avoidance conflict. In other words, she wants to avoid both babysitting her younger sister and spending the evening with her parents. It is simply picking between the lesser of two evils. In an approach-approach conflict, a person likes both choices and has to pick the best of the best. In an approach-avoidance conflict, an individual both likes and dislikes a choice.

25. B: Criteria for generalized anxiety disorder specifies excessive worry about a number of events or activities as opposed to an isolated fear or concern. Further, it tends to persist for long periods rather than having an abrupt onset. Somatization disorder is characterized by complaints regarding several organ systems involving different body sites and functions, rather a single body organ. Post-traumatic stress disorder requires confronting an event or events that involve actual or threatened death or serious injury. The client was away at school, did not witness his father's death, and it didn't pose any direct threat to him. Panic attacks involve sudden onset, profound fear of death, and other symptoms such as those the client has described.

26. D: John Bowlby was of a psychoanalytic mindset, believing that early experiences had an impact on development and further shaped who one was to become in later life. He theorized that attachment behavior is instinctive, and further formed through the relationship one has as an infant with the primary caregiver. Bowlby also saw an evolutionary element in attachment in that it aids in the individual's ability to survive. He saw problems in infant/childhood attachment as a precursor to other problems in later life. He suggested such issues as delinquency, depression, aggression, affectionless psychopathy, and lowered levels of intelligence as possible problems one might suffer later in life as a result of maternal deprivation.

27. A: Negative reinforcement involves the taking away of something undesirable so that the desirable behavior is increased. Positive reinforcement involves receiving something desirable when the positive behavior is performed. For example, a child does his homework so that his mom

Copyright © Mometrix Media. You have been licensed one copy of this document for personal use only. Any other reproduction or redistribution is strictly prohibited. All rights reserved.

will stop nagging him about doing it (positive behavior increases by taking away a reinforcer). Or, a child gets to watch a few extra minutes of a cartoon because he did his homework (increases positive behavior by adding a reinforcer).

28. D: A t-score has a mean of 50 and a standard deviation of 10. This should not be confused with an IQ score. An IQ score has a mean of 100 and a standard deviation of 15. A z-score expresses the number of standard deviations that a raw score is from the mean.

29. C: Carl Roger's client-centered approach to therapy mirrors back what the patient is saying, guiding him/her to clearer self-understanding. Rogers believed in freeing clients from obstacles to growth, and aiding them in becoming independent, self-directed individuals. This type of therapy involves a therapist who is more facilitator than director, and only guides clients in making their own decisions. The Rogerian approach involves a positive outlook and high degrees of respect for the client. This type of therapy works well with many types of cases, but is often not the best choice for more severe disorders, such as schizophrenia or other organic disorders.

30. A: Disengagement means being uninvolved in social interactions. Therefore, this is an example of someone disengaged from their family. Enmeshment is when family members are over-involved in the lives of other family members. "Placater" is a term used in Satir's conjoint family therapy to describe a person who tries to please everyone. Triangulation occurs in families when several family members gang up on one particular family member.

31. C: If, when working with prospective employers about hiring those with mental disabilities, an employer asks the counselor if it is legal to ask potential employees if they are disabled during the initial interview, the best response is: "You may ask only if the person can perform job functions." If the individual is able to carry out the job functions, the individual is under no obligation to provide information about a disability. However, the individual may choose to divulge a disability and ask for workplace accommodations.

32. A: If a client in a support group assumes that another member of the group who is hearing impaired is also intellectually disabled, the correct description of this attitude is the halo effect. The halo effect occurs when one suggests that the unrelated physical characteristics or disabilities of a person somehow attribute to a negative characteristic, such as intellectual disability, even though there is no evidence that this is, in fact, true.

33. C: Individuals who have been diagnosed with severe mental illness, have histories of being violent or explosive, have limited cognitive or thinking abilities, are unable to communicate effectively, or use alcohol or other recreational drugs are not good candidates for inclusion in a group. It is important for all group members to feel safe, and having an individual who is prone to violence in the group may compromise safety. It is also important that all group members effectively communicate, process, and understand interpersonal relationships at a functional level. Therefore, individuals with limited capacities for any of these skills would not be good candidates for inclusion in a group. The process of a group is to learn and practice more appropriate social interaction skills. Someone who is incapable of understanding social interaction skills would not be a good candidate for the group.

34. D: Malpractice claims almost exclusively deal with a counselor's behavior that ends up harming the client in some way. Negligence on the part of the counselor could lead to potential harm to the client. Of course, any physical or psychological injury to a client harms the client. If there never was a professional relationship established, then the counselor cannot be sued for malpractice. A professional relationship is established usually within the first few sessions and involves informed

Copyright © Mometrix Media. You have been licensed one copy of this document for personal use only. Any other reproduction or redistribution is strictly prohibited. All rights reserved.

consent, discussion of the limits of confidentiality, and the process of therapy. If these components were not established early on in the relationship, then there really is no professional relationship.

35. C: Abraham Maslow is associated with existentialism and Carl Rogers is considered a humanist. Sigmund Freud is associated with psychoanalysis or psychodynamics. Carl Jung is a Neo-Freudian.

36. A: The Rorschach is an inkblot test. The TAT (Thematic Apperception Test) is a storytelling test. The Rotters Incomplete Sentences test is a finish-the-sentence test. All of these tests are projective tests because they ask test takers to project their own thoughts and ideas into the stimuli to complete the answers. The test takers come up with their own answers freely without any suggestions or information being provided by the examiner except the stimuli. Rating scales are typically used to describe various dimensions of behavior across a number of different situations or environments. Standardized personality tests include the MMPI-II and CPI, among others. Observational tests would typically involve the examiner observing the test takers' behavior across environments or situations.

37. D: B. F. Skinner believed that behavior is determined from external factors rather than from internal issues. He theorized that reinforcements can be used to control behavior, and that punishment was one of the ways that behavior could be modified. However, Skinner believed that punishment was not the best technique for behavior modification. He felt that an individual will work harder, and learn faster, when positive reinforcement is used. He theorized that there are many alternatives to the use of punishment as a reinforcer, and that those options should take precedence when possible.

38. C: The Social Distance Scale is a technique developed by Emory Bogardus in the 1930s to measure social distance. It's usually thought of as related to issues of prejudice. The scale asks an individual to agree or disagree with a number of statements about a particular group. It looks at factors such as intimacy, warmth, hostility, and indifference. The scale measures a person's willingness to connect socially with different groups depending upon their social closeness to someone from that group. Bogardus found negative attitudes toward Turks, African-Americans, and Jewish and Mexican groups in his study. A replication of the study in 1947 found that those attitudes were still present.

39. C: A statement of disclosure is not required by law in every state of the U.S., but may be required in some states. Since it is required by law in some states, answer B is incorrect. A statement of disclosure is given to a potential or new client before counseling begins, so answer D is incorrect.

40. B: Ethical dilemmas related to confidentiality issues arise more often than those involving dual relationships, credentials of test administrators, or licensure. These issues of confidentially may or may not be intentional and are commonly committed mistakenly. Nonetheless the consequences for breaches in confidentiality, whether intentional or mistakenly, are very serious and must be carefully considered.

41. C: A code of ethics is not a legal and binding document, nor is it a set of strict rules by which counselors must abide. It is really a guideline or a set of standards for best professional and moral conduct. There usually are no right or wrong answers to ethical dilemmas. When confronted with an ethical dilemma, discuss it with other counselors and/or contact the ethics committee.

42. C: Culture-bound values in counseling include the following: individually centered therapy; verbal, emotional, and behavioral expressiveness; defined communication patterns; openness, and intimacy. Class-bound values in counseling include strict adherence to a time schedule; ambiguous

Copyright © Mometrix Media. You have been licensed one copy of this document for personal use only. Any other reproduction or redistribution is strictly prohibited. All rights reserved.

or unstructured approaches to problems; and, looking for long-range solutions or setting long-range goals. Answers A, B, and D are all reversed (i.e., elements of culture-bound values are identified as belonging to class-bound values, and vice versa).

43. D: If a counselor plans to close his practice, he must inform all of his clients of that fact, provide the clients with referrals to other professionals, and notify all clients of the safeguards for the clinical records. If these procedures are not followed, the counselor could be violating ethical standards by abandoning his clients. Simply calling the patients and notifying them of this change is not ethical.

44. C: The **Addiction Severity Index (ASI)** includes questions about socioeconomic status and psychological needs as well as the use of addictive substances. The **CAGE** tool is a 4-questions self-assessment of alcohol use. The **CAGE-AID** tool is similar but includes the use of drugs. The **Alcohol Use Disorders Identification Test (AUDIT)** includes 10 questions about drinking habits and how it affects the client's life. **AUDIT**-C is a 3-question modification of the AUDIT.

45. B: Purposeful sampling is only used when there is NO interest in generalizing the research findings to the population because it is not randomized. Purposeful sampling may be comprehensive, may involve extreme-case selection, or it may consist of typical-case selection.

46. D: Asian children usually have lower self-esteem than their North American counterparts, while African American children have higher self-esteem than their Caucasian counterparts. Generally, boys have higher self-esteem than girls. An authoritative parenting style is generally more accepting and less critical of children's negative behavior: Parents tend to build their children's self-esteem because the focus is on building a sense of worth and independence.

47. D: Haley's strategic family therapy describes the role of the therapist as finding the myths that keep behavior going, understanding levels of communication, and focusing on levels of organization in families. Overcoming feelings of inferiority is part of the Adlerian family therapy.

48. C: Reliability levels of 0.60 or below are often considered to be too low to be acceptable. Lower levels can be acceptable only if the counselor is using the information gained from the test in conjunction with other tests or information and should not be considered if the counselor is using it as the primary source of information about the client. A high reliability is considered 0.90, with 0.80 as moderate and 0.70 as low reliability. A reliability of 0.60 would be considered by most to be too low to be of significant use.

49. C: Rater bias refers to a supervisor's bias in how employees are rated. With the "horns" type of bias, one negative attribute of the employee causes the supervisor to rate everything about that employee more negatively. There are other types of bias also, including leniency, halo, severity, stereotyping, recency, similarity, negative effect, and comparison. Ideally, supervisors will rate their employees in an accurate, realistic manner. However, rater bias can happen, either consciously or unconsciously. When it does happen, it can be costly to both employees and companies, so identifying it, and dealing with it, can be a critical concern.

50. B: When counseling a client who is self-identified as a lesbian and whom the counselor believes is marginalized, the first step should be to determine if the client feels marginalized. It's important to avoid making assumptions about others. If the client does not feel marginalized, then focusing on marginalization may avoid the real issues that are concerning the client and may, in fact, increase the client's level of stress by introducing new areas of conflict that the client had not previously experienced.

Copyright © Mometrix Media. You have been licensed one copy of this document for personal use only. Any other reproduction or redistribution is strictly prohibited. All rights reserved.

51. D: When group members hear different feedback from each co-leader, it may stimulate the energy of the group and lead to more multi-faceted discussions, which can enhance the group process. Co-leaders should not always have the same amount of experience, because co-leading is a good way to help newer, less experienced group leaders by pairing them with a more experienced co-leader. Co-leaders should not be of the same sex, as it is often more helpful if a male and a female are paired as co-leaders. For example, two men might be too competitive, and two women might be too cooperative. Thus, the dynamic between a male and a female would likely be more balanced and more likely to introduce discussion-stimulating differences in views. Co-leaders should have a good working relationship. Therefore, having markedly different theoretical orientations that could induce conflict is not a good idea.

52. D: It is expected that all counselors respect diversity in their clients and educate themselves as to the individualistic needs of the clients as affected by such concepts as social identity, history, and economic and political issues, as relevant to particular cultures. Respect for individual cultures and knowledge of their unique and special features are necessary for a counselor to responsibly and ethically provide competent service to their clients.

53. C: A client's dislike of a counselor's methods or techniques is NOT a criterion for filing a malpractice suit in court. As long as the methods are not inappropriate or unprofessional, malpractice cannot be established. If the client does not like the counselor's approach, the client should seek a different therapist. The conditions for a malpractice claim to succeed are: professional relationship was established; there was a breach of duty; the client suffered physical or psychological injury; and the injury was caused by the breach of duty.

54. A: If a client maintains the same sad expression throughout the entire psychosocial assessment, the client's affect would be described as **restricted** because the client showed only one expression. A **flat** affect is characterized by no expression. An **inappropriate** affect occurs when the facial expression does not match the mood or situation. A **blunted** affect is one in which the individual shows little expression or in which the expressions respond slowly to mood or situation.

55. D: If a mental health client is making statements that seem to be based on delusional thinking, the best way to express doubt is, "That's hard to believe." This statement is not overtly challenging but does avoid reinforcing false beliefs and may help to undermine the client's faulty belief system. The counselor should avoid arguing with the client or directly confronting the client's false statements, as this is rarely effective, but should remain calm and try to reset reality.

56. A: A culture-specific disorder is one that is typical of a given culture. Culture shock is stress induced by living in a different culture. Culture free refers to a test whose score is not dependent on knowledge specific to a given culture. Cross-cultural means crossing more than one culture.

57. B: Freud described some of the unconscious processes that individuals use to protect themselves from conflicts and anxiety. These unconscious processes are called defense mechanisms, with the most important being repression. Repression occurs when a threatening memory, idea, or emotion is blocked from consciousness. Regression is a defense mechanism that occurs when a person reverts to a previous phase of psychological development. Denial occurs when a person refuses to admit that something unpleasant is happening. Finally, reaction formation occurs when an individual transforms his/her unconscious anxiety into its opposite outwardly.

58. C: An adult student, as the one described in this question, is given the same rights that any adult is given. The student has the right to view his educational records without the consent of his parents, as he is an adult. The Family Educational Rights and Privacy Act affords him the right to

Copyright © Mometrix Media. You have been licensed one copy of this document for personal use only. Any other reproduction or redistribution is strictly prohibited. All rights reserved.

have access to his own records. If the student was under the age of 18, parental permission would be required.

59. B: If a client has sat in the same chair with the right arm extended for an hour after the phlebotomist extended the arm for a blood draw, this is an example of waxy flexibility, a psychomotor behavior associated with schizophrenia with catatonia. With waxy flexibility, the client maintains a position initiated by someone else (such as the phlebotomist). This differs from posturing in that, with posturing, the client voluntarily assumes abnormal or bizarre postures.

60. A: The gold stars Harry receives are tokens. He gets to purchase rewards—privileges or items he values—with the tokens he receives for performing desired behaviors. A token economy is a type of behavior modification used for shaping behavior. A reinforcement schedule is a behavioral term referring to the criteria for giving reinforcements or rewards. It may relate to time or to number of occurrences (i.e., an interval schedule or a ratio schedule), and it may be fixed or variable. Systematic desensitization is another behavioral technique used to reduce unpleasant reactions to specific stimuli. This technique of counterconditioning, based on the theory of reciprocal inhibition, pairs the triggering stimulus with more pleasant events so that the client's association with that stimulus changes from negative to positive. It is useful with phobias, some anxiety disorders, and other learned negative responses. Negative reinforcement is also a behavioral term. It refers to removing a favored stimulus (NOT to introducing a punishment).

61. B: Umwelt means the world of the physical or biological system. Mitwelt refers to the world of relationships. Eigenwelt is the world of self-identity. (Welt means world in German. Um means around and umwelt means environment. Mit means with, so Mitwelt refers to one's relationships with others. Eigen means one's own, so Eigenwelt is one's own world or the self.)

62. B: One of Lazarus' modalities is sensations (i.e., vision, hearing, smell, taste, and touch). However, a perception is not a sensation, but rather the interpretation of a sensation. Further, the clarification that the perception is of a nonexistent odor suggests that it is either a hallucination or an aura (which some people experience preceding a migraine or seizure). Lazarus' seven modalities spell out the acronym BASIC ID. The acronym represents: behaviors; affective responses (emotions, moods); sensations; images (memories, dreams, and how we see ourselves); cognitions (ideas, thoughts); interpersonal relationships; and drugs (i.e., biology, including nutrition). The act of standing up or sitting down is a behavior. Having a conversation with an acquaintance is an interpersonal relationship experience (i.e., engaging in interactions with people). Having an idea about how to solve a problem involves cognition (an idea, thought, philosophy or insight).

63. C: An example of feedback that is directed at an action that the client cannot modify is "You have memory problems because of your alcohol abuse" because the client cannot undue the physical damage that has been caused by any specific action. The client can modify behavior based on the other feedback. The client can modify behavior if the client has made an inappropriate comment, can control or explore the reasons for anger, and can also attempt to make eye contact with the son during a subsequent visit.

64. C: Multiple-choice questions of any sort tap into a person's recognition memory. The person is given information from which to choose the correct answer. Recall is tapped using short-answer essays or a fill-in-the-blank format. Test takers are provided with very little information and must rely on their own recall memory to retrieve the answers. Organization and planning have no relevance here.

Copyright © Mometrix Media. You have been licensed one copy of this document for personal use only. Any other reproduction or redistribution is strictly prohibited. All rights reserved.

65. B: If an adolescent male is seeing the counselor after he was arrested along with four other boys for breaking into a school and vandalizing it as part of an initiation into a club and states he was aware that what he was doing was wrong but didn't questions and went along with the group anyway, this is an example of deindividuation. Being immersed in a group caused the client to be less aware of his own sense of value and to do things that he would likely not have done by himself.

66. D: If a counselor decides to administer a psychological test, most likely the counselor wants to understand the client more fully. The counselor may want to predict the future performance of a client. Or the counselor may want to evaluate the outcomes of treatment. A psychological test provides a means to look at these issues objectively and concretely.

67. A: If a therapy group for women who have suffered intimate partner violence has agreed to avoid making negative comments about each other, but during one discussion, one member tells another, "You are a complete idiot if you believe your husband is going to change his behavior!" the most appropriate response is, "I can see you are concerned, but we have agreed to avoid negative comments about each other." Instead of blaming or pointing the finger, this acknowledges the client's feelings while still pointing out the violation.

68. C: If a client worries about how she looks, checks her appearance in the mirror repeatedly for 4 to 5 hours every day, has had repeated plastic surgical procedures, and is diagnosed with body dysmorphic disorder and prescribed an SSRI by a psychiatrist, the approach to therapy that is most indicated is cognitive restructuring. Cognitive restructuring focuses on feelings that result in stress and asks the client to determine what is true about the feelings and what is false and then to develop alternative thoughts.

69. A: This is typical of a level 1 response (i.e., a response that does not attend to or detracts significantly from the client's affect). In this example, the client is obviously very upset and expresses it. The counselor then responds with a simple, concrete question not reflecting the client's affect. A level 2 response is one that subtracts noticeably from the client's affect, and might be something like, "You seem a bit perturbed." A level 3 response is one that is interchangeable with the client's affect, and might be something like, "My goodness! You certainly are very upset about how she yelled at you." A level 4 or 5 response is one that adds noticeably (4) or significantly (5) to the client's affect, and might be, "I can see that you're really upset at how she yelled at you. Your feelings are terribly hurt by what she said and how she said it, and you feel crushed and destroyed by it. It has damaged your self-esteem and your relationship."

70. D: Career counselors are involved in all of these activities. They help clients become better aware of themselves, teach decision-making skills, and teach employability skills.

71. B: Workaholism is a term that is widely used, but not well defined. It refers to someone who has an over commitment to work that is not related to external needs. It is generally viewed that there are two types of workaholic, one that likes his work and the other who doesn't like his work. A workaholic who does not like his work is more likely to experience problems as a result. There are also more likely to be problems for the workaholic who has a family-work conflict because of the over-attention to work. This is an increased area of interest in recent years.

72. D: Hypnosis is, simply put, a deep state of relaxation in which the client is not quite awake and not quite asleep. It is a trance-like, in-between state. During this state, the client is more open to suggestion and sometimes better able to utilize recall of various events. Many people believe that hypnosis is only a magician's trick, or if legitimate at all, useful only for memory recall or

Copyright © Mometrix Media. You have been licensed one copy of this document for personal use only. Any other reproduction or redistribution is strictly prohibited. All rights reserved.

psychological issues. However, hypnosis is often used today to treat such medical issues as asthma, chronic pain, easing childbirth, lowering blood pressure, and many others.

73. C: Sigmund Freud's psychosexual stages of development consist of five stages. The second stage, the "Anal Stage," is when the focus is on the anus and the child's sexual gratification is derived from bowel movements. In the "Phallic Stage," the child is fascinated with the penis (or for girls, the lack of). The "Latency Stage" brings with it a period of calm and little conflict, and the "Genital Stage" brings a postpuberty focus on the genitals, maturity, creation of life, and creativity. However, it is the first stage, the "Oral Stage," in which the smoker from our question is likely to be fixated. It is in the Oral Stage that the mouth/sucking is the primary location of pleasure for the individual.

74. A: To Raymond Cattell, personality is about being able to predict an individual's behavior in any given situation. Part of this is an understanding that the components of an individual's personality are made up of "source traits," which one can only identify through "factor analysis." This is not to be confused with "surface traits" that are personality characteristics resulting from two or more source traits. Surface traits are not a basic component of personality. Also, not to be confused is the term "unique trait," which simply refers to a trait that is unique to an individual and not shared by others.

75. C: Occupational stress refers to stress that is related specifically to the vocational situation. This stress can be affected by issues such as the type of work itself, as well as its relation to the skill set of the individual. It may also relate to the work environment, relationships with coworkers, organizational climate, perceptions and realistic expectations, number of hours worked each week, etc. Research into occupational stress raises questions about its relation to the immune system and general health. This concern is not only significant because of the implications for the individual, but also for society in general (as it increases the cost of health care and loss of productivity for companies).

76. B: Behavioral techniques, employ techniques of classical and operant conditioning (reinforcement, shaping, extinction) as well as systematic desensitization, implosion, flooding, time-out, and thought stopping. In psychoanalysis, the counselor relies on free association, dream analysis, analysis of transferences, and interpretation to advance therapy progress. A counselor who uses TA (transactional analysis) uses interrogation, confrontation, illustration, and concentration on early memories to assist clients. The reality therapist uses humor, confrontation, role modeling, role playing, and defining limits.

77. A: Communication patterns generally look at what is said, while meta-communication looks at how something is said in terms of nonverbal communication techniques and motivations.

78. A: According to Title II and Title III of the Americans with Disabilities Act, an emotional comfort animal does not qualify as a service animal. Service animals must actually provide some type of active service and must be canine although special requests can be made to qualify miniature horses. Psychiatric services dogs, on the other hand, are qualified and may be trained to identify oncoming psychiatric episodes, remind the client to take medications, interrupt self-injurious behavior, or protect disoriented clients from danger.

79. A: The unpredictability of an intermittent schedule of reinforcement makes it the hardest to extinguish because the subject doesn't know if he will get reinforced the next time or in five minutes or after twenty tries. All the other schedules of reinforcement are predictable.

80. C: The Hamilton Rating Scale for Depression (HAM-D) is completed by the observer and is intended to determine the severity of diagnosed depression. The items on the scale are scored from

Copyright © Mometrix Media. You have been licensed one copy of this document for personal use only. Any other reproduction or redistribution is strictly prohibited. All rights reserved.

0 to 4 or 0 to 2, depending on the nature of the item. The seventeen items included for evaluation of depression include depressed mood; guilt; suicide; initial, middle, and delayed insomnia; work and interest; retardation; agitation: psychic and somatic anxiety; somatic (gastrointestinal); somatic (general); genital; hypochondriasis; insight; and weight loss. Four other items are assessed for general information: diurnal variation, depersonalization, paranoia, and obsessional symptoms.

81. B: If a client was involved in a severe accident that result in the death of the client's spouse and child, but the client has been unable to recall anything about the accident, the client is likely experiencing **localized amnesia**, which usually occurs in response to severe trauma and persists for hours or days. **Selective amnesia** involves the inability to remember some aspects of a traumatic event while remembering other aspects. **Generalized amnesia** is the inability to recall anything at all for the lifetime of the person. **Systematized amnesia** is the inability to recall a particular category or type of memory, such as one event or person.

82. D: Informed consent is the practice of providing the client with all the information so that he or she may agree to or reject treatment, testing, or interventions. Informed consent involves discussing the process of therapy, the limits of confidentiality, possible outcomes of therapy (positive and negative), any risks to the client, and clinic procedures for billing and missed appointments. Informed consent is given in writing.

83. C: The Career Pattern Study was a study by Donald Super that investigated the vocational behavior of individuals from 9th grade into their 30s. He found that career maturity and achievement in high school were predictive of the same behaviors in adulthood. The Vocational Preference Inventory and the Self-Directed Search were both developed by John Holland for identifying a person's predominant vocational personality type according to his typology. The Career Assessment Inventory is an instrument developed by Charles B. Johansson, which adopted Holland's typology. The Strong Interest Inventory is another instrument in which Strong also used Holland's typology.

84. A: The WAIS is the Wechsler Adult Intelligence Scale for those over the age of sixteen, and it is the IQ test for adults. It was developed by David Wechsler and began in 1939 as the Wechsler-Bellevue Scale. In 1955, the WAIS replaced that original test, and has gone through several revisions since that time. The eleven subtests of the WAIS address both verbal (six subtests) and performance (five subtests) abilities. The subject receives scaled scores for each of the subtests, and then an overall performance IQ score, verbal IQ score, and a full-scale IQ (FSIQ) score.

85. A: In Freudian psychoanalysis, dream analysis is a psychotherapeutic technique used to interpret the client's dreams. Freud believed that dreams contain information about unconscious thoughts and conflicts that can be useful in treating the client. "Manifest content" is the term given for the conscious (or remembered) parts of the dream. "Latent content" is unconscious (not remembered) material from the dream. Psychoanalysts analyze the manifest content (in an attempt to get at the latent content) as a way to better understand the inner workings of the client's mind, especially material that might be sexual or aggressive in nature.

86. D: If a client has difficulty with both verbal and nonverbal communication that is appropriate for the social context, is unable to match communication to the needs of the listener, and has difficulty recognizing clues for turn-taking but exhibits no additional behavior associated with autism spectrum disorder, these symptoms are characteristic of social (pragmatic) communication disorder. Autism spectrum disorder is characterized by more intense verbal and nonverbal communication problems as well as repetitive motor movements, fixated interests, and abnormal response to sensory input, with the level depending on the degree of severity.

Copyright © Mometrix Media. You have been licensed one copy of this document for personal use only. Any other reproduction or redistribution is strictly prohibited. All rights reserved.

87. A: One of the most widely studied aspects of altruism is the question of why one person helps a person in need when another will not. The "bystander effect" says that people are more likely to help someone in need if no one else is present. Many studies of bystander intervention show that the majority of people will step in to help someone if there is no one else around to do so. Possible explanations for this effect are that people may look to others for information on how to act, or they may feel the other will act for them.

88. C: When counseling a client with PTSD, the counselor should advise the client to talk about problems with support people, such as close friends, family, or members of a support group. Avoidance strategies usually work for only limited periods of time and are not helpful in recovery because the client is not dealing effectively with the issue. Clients with PTSD can practice relaxation techniques as well, but they may need to do so in small increments of time initially.

89. A: A structured group focuses on a central theme, which could be drinking/driving issues, dealing with loss and/or grief, anger management, learning job seeking skills and the like. A structured group has a leader. A self-help group has no leader and is a support system to help with psychological stress. A self-help group may also focus on loss or grief, weight loss, incest survivors, or parents who have lost a child. A psychoeducation group focuses on acquiring information and building skills for coping with disorders. It can be preventive, growth-oriented, or remedial in nature. Psychoeducation groups are often held at social service or mental health agencies and universities. A T-group, or training group, focuses on improving interpersonal skills. They often study the way a person functions in a group such as in a work environment.

90. D: RCMAS assesses anxiety in children and adolescents (6-19) with 37 yes-no questions and can be read to young children. **HAS** provides an evaluation of overall anxiety and its degree of severity for children and adults. This scale is frequently utilized in psychotropic drug evaluations. **BAI** is a tool for adolescents and adults that ranks 21 common symptoms related to anxiety, according to the degree they have bothered the client in the previous month. **BDI** is a widely utilized, self-reported, multiple-choice questionnaire consisting of 21 items, which measures the degree of depression for those 17 to 80 years.

91. C: Construct validity exists when a test successfully measures a hypothetical construct, such as locus of control, field dependency, creativity, etc. Convergent validation occurs when the construct being studied correlates highly with other constructs. Discriminant validation occurs when there is no statistically significant correlation with other constructs. Content validity refers to the instrument containing items from the proper domain of usable items. Predictive validity refers to the confirmation of a test's predictions by later behaviors or other measurable criteria. Concurrent validity refers to test results being successfully compared with other criteria or test results at the same time.

92. D: If a client expresses great anxiety and fears about an upcoming meeting with her employer, and the counselor asks, "What is the worst thing that can happen?", the approach that the counselor is utilizing is decatastrophizing, a cognitive restructuring technique used to treat a client's cognitive distortions, such as catastrophizing during which the client exaggerates the severity of a problem or assumes that the worst possible outcome will occur.

93. B: There is a normal score distribution. One would use a nonparametric test when they are NOT able assume that the distribution of scores resembles a normal curve. If there is a normal distribution, parametric tests (such as analyses of variance or correlational tests) can be used. Nonparametric tests are indicated if: 1) the sample's variance is similar to the population's variance (i.e., the sample is homogeneous); 2) if data is collected from two samples which are independent of

Copyright © Mometrix Media. You have been licensed one copy of this document for personal use only. Any other reproduction or redistribution is strictly prohibited. All rights reserved.

one another, in which case the Mann-Whitney U test could be used; or, 3) if data are nominal (i.e., they are in groups or categories, such as male and female). In this case, a Chi-square test could be used to see whether the two distributions have a significant difference.

94. C: Reinforcement increases the likelihood of a behavior occurring again, and punishment decreases the likelihood of the behavior occurring again. Reinforcements are positive and desirable, so an individual will perform behaviors to get them. Punishments are negative and undesirable, so an individual will avoid performing certain behaviors so they don't get punished.

95. A: What is normal (or abnormal) can certainly be debated, but in psychology, "abnormal" behavior is generally viewed as behavior that is maladaptive and harmful. If the behavior is harmful to the self or others and/or causing significant difficulties in the individual's life, then the behavior may be termed abnormal. In the medical model, abnormality is due to an illness, but psychology takes a broader view than this. The Diagnostic and Statistical Manual of Mental Disorders (DSM), published by the American Psychiatric Association, contains definitions and classifications of mental disorders, which aids in the determination of what is to be considered "normal."

96. A: Test bias refers to anything within a test that is unfair to an individual or group, such as asking questions about Wisconsin to people who live in Australia and who have never been in Wisconsin. In this example, the test developer could minimize test bias by developing norms for Australians who take the test and using those norms when an Australian takes the Wisconsin test. Answers B, C, and D may be only minimally helpful in eliminating or minimizing bias in testing.

97. B: A placebo is a substance that is generally used in one of two ways. It can be used as a control in an experiment to determine the true effectiveness of a medication. A placebo can also be used as a substitute for a medication, and is meant to work based on the expectation of the subject using the placebo. Many studies have shown that giving a placebo is preferable to providing no treatment at all, and that many patients favorably respond to placebos. Some professionals believe that the use of placebos is unprofessional, and its use in psychotherapy is controversial. However, even though not completely understood, it has been shown to be beneficial in some cases.

98. B: The Myers-Briggs Type Indicator (MBTI) is a test based upon the theory of Carl Jung, and measures personality types. It looks at sixteen distinct personality types. The test is considered to be both valid and reliable, and is very simple to administer. The MBTI does not make judgments about the different types of personalities, but rather is a means by which to understand the differences and similarities among types of people. Analysis of the test can be useful to the client in terms of issues such as self-awareness, career choice, and personal relationships.

99. B: If a client who is an airline pilot is facing mandatory retirement and reports feeling increasing stress and anxiety because his retirement income is considerably less than his current income, he still has young children from a second marriage, and he is unsure what he will do with his time and is unsure of his job skills, the adjunctive service that may most benefit the client is vocational counseling. Since his income will fall, the client may need to consider alternate work plans but may need help in determining how to apply the skills he has learned as a pilot.

100. B: Problem use. Stages of substance abuse:

1. **Experimentation**: Use is occasional, socially or in response to stress.
2. **Regular use**: A regular pattern of use, in response to specific stressors.
3. **Problem use**: Problems occur because of substance abuse—loss of job, social exclusion, physical impairments/injuries, depression, motor vehicle accidents, and/or failing grades.

Copyright © Mometrix Media. You have been licensed one copy of this document for personal use only. Any other reproduction or redistribution is strictly prohibited. All rights reserved.

4. **Dependence**: Chronic use despite problems and risks and exhibits increasing tolerance and begins to experience withdrawal with decreased use.
5. **Addiction**: Physical and psychological need for the substance, despite problems it is causing, exhibits cravings and alcohol/drug seeking behaviors, including lying and stealing.

101. B: A test may be reliable, meaning it is consistent and its results can be replicated, without being valid, meaning it does not test what it claims to test. Answer A is the definition of reliability, not validity. Answer C is not true because valid tests will normally be reliable (unless the variable being measured changes). Answer D is not true of reliability but is true of validity, which is situation-specific (i.e., a test can be valid for some purposes but not for others).

102. B: Changes in human growth and development that are viewed as qualitative are changes in structure or organization (i.e. biological or sexual development). Changes in number, degree, or frequency are viewed as quantitative or as changes in content (i.e. intellectual development). Changes that are sequential are viewed as continuous and cannot be easily separated. Changes that are discontinuous can be separated from others (i.e. language development) and these fit readily into stage theories of development.

103. B: The Minnesota Importance Questionnaire (MIQ) is a useful tool in vocational counseling. The MIQ measures twenty psychological needs and six underlying values as related to work satisfaction, and it includes 185 occupations. The six values from which the needs are derived are achievement, comfort, status, autonomy, safety, and altruism. The test is a paper-and-pencil inventory, gender neutral, and appropriate for those who are reading at a fifth-grade level or higher. It can be administered to groups or individuals. A Spanish language edition of the MIQ is also available.

104. C: Albert Bandura stressed imitation, modeling, and observation as the key components in learning. His most famous experiment took place in 1961. It involved showing a group of children a film of a woman beating and shouting angrily at a Bobo doll. The children were then allowed to play in a room that included a Bobo doll, and they would interact with the doll in an aggressive manner, as was modeled for them in the film. Bandura felt this indicated that we learn not just by reinforcement (as behavioral theory suggested), but also by simple observation.

105. D: Down syndrome is a common genetic condition causing mental and physical impairment. The most common form is called trisomy 21, which involves an extra copy of the 21st chromosome. There have been many medical and social advances in regards to Down syndrome over the past several years. Many Down syndrome children are now living longer and integrated into the school systems and communities. The physical features and impairments of each case vary significantly, as does intellectual ability. Some require a great deal of supervision and special service, while others may lead relatively healthy and involved lives.

106. B: While many students seek out career counseling, those that are least likely come from low income families, possibly broken families, where their role is caretaker of younger siblings because their parent(s) are unable to do so due to incapacities or juggling several minimum wage jobs. It is important to empower these students to pursue their own career aspirations despite their responsibilities at home.

107. C: If a client who recently learned he had kidney cancer has been researching everything he can about the disease, treatment, and outlook, the defense mechanism the client is utilizing is **intellectualism**, examining all the facts in a straightforward manner in order to avoid an emotional reaction. **Rationalization** is explaining unacceptable thoughts or behavior in a positive light.

Copyright © Mometrix Media. You have been licensed one copy of this document for personal use only. Any other reproduction or redistribution is strictly prohibited. All rights reserved.

Repression is a mental process that removes thoughts and emotions from consciousness. **Compensation** is the act of overachieving in one way in order to make up for lack of achievement in another.

108. A: AIMS is a tool to evaluate tardive dyskinesia in those taking antipsychotic medications. The **CAGE** tool is used as a quick assessment tool to determine if people are drinking excessively or are problem drinkers. **MMSE** is used to assess cognition in those with evidence of dementia or short-term memory loss, often associated with Alzheimer's disease. The **Confusion Assessment Method** is used to assess the development of delirium and is intended primarily for those without psychiatric training.

109. C: A variety of roles are seen in group therapy dynamics. These roles often assist in the proper performance of the group. The "gatekeeper" is a type of "maintenance" role within the group. Maintenance roles address the socio-emotional aspects of the entire group. In terms of the gatekeeper specifically, he/she is the group member who organizes and leads. He/she may also encourage other members of the group, making sure they each get a chance to speak their mind, and keep communication open. Other common "maintenance" roles within the group are the Harmonizer, Supporter, and Compromiser, among others.

110. D: Because a client in early stages of recovery must deal with the stress of maintaining sobriety, the client is likely to be most successful if initial jobs are less demanding than those previously held. The goal is for the client to develop self-esteem from working, good work habits, and a history of steady employment. The client may need to move through a series of jobs before being ready to return to the initial field of work.

111. A: Someone who is nonassertive within the group therapy setting is quite the same as someone who is nonassertive in other situations. The goal of the passive, nonassertive individual is to avoid conflict and be liked by others. For this reason, the nonassertive person is likely to agree with what others say, or at least give the impression that he does. This type of interaction may serve to avoid and/or diffuse conflict. However, others in the group may not always react positively toward the nonassertive individual because they have a hard time knowing what the nonassertive person really feels and believes, and they also may not respect the nonassertive person because of his/her passive behavior.

112. B: When one member of a group begins to exhibit negative nonverbal communication (such as eye-rolling or looking bored), the counselor, who is serving as the group leader, routinely directs the group's attention toward another member of the group by asking the other group member a question or making a comment, this best exemplifies blocking. Blocking is an action taken to interrupt inappropriate comments or behavior or when a group member's emotions are overwhelming the individual. The group leader must find a way to redirect attention without shaming or blaming the member to who the blocking is directed.

113. B: The Social Exchange Theory reduces altruism to the simple factors of cost and gain. The theory says that people do things for those people from whom they can expect something in return. Of course, this theory does not explain all instances of altruistic behavior, but it does point to the reason for some altruistic acts. In fact, some professionals theorize that there is no such thing as a purely altruistic act.

Copyright © Mometrix Media. You have been licensed one copy of this document for personal use only. Any other reproduction or redistribution is strictly prohibited. All rights reserved.

114. A: With alcohol addiction, the client may begin exhibiting beginning withdrawal within 8 hours. Withdrawal stages:

1. **Beginning withdrawal:** Usually within 8 hours: tremors, abdominal cramping, anorexia, general weakness, nausea and vomiting, excessive sweating, irritability, mood swings, and depression.
2. **Withdrawal:** Usually within 24 hours: In addition to stage one symptoms, increased anxiety and mood swings, increased blood pressure and the respiratory rate, urinary and fecal incontinence, muscle rigidity, and clenching of teeth.
3. **Severe withdrawal:** Varies from 12 hours to up to 14 days, extreme confusion with hallucinations. severe agitation, seizure, and life-threatening *delirium tremens* with circulatory collapse and death.

115. C: Denial: Completely refusing to acknowledge a situation that is stressful, such as ignoring a son's probable drug problem. **Intellectualism**: Using rational intellectual processes to deal with stress and loss, such as by discussing positive aspects of being single. **Displacement**: Transferring feelings from one person or thing to another, such as being angry with a boss and taking the anger out on a spouse. **Rationalization**: Attempting to find excuses for unacceptable behavior or feelings, such as drinking to relieve the stress of work.

116. A: The National Vocational Guidance Association founded in 1913 is known as the first professional counseling association. Though the Vocation Bureau in Boston, directed by Frank Parsons, began earlier in 1908, it is not known as the first professional counseling association. The APGA founded in 1951 and the OVR founded in 1954 were both founded later than the NVGA.

117. C: The Minnesota Job Description Questionnaire (MJDQ) is an assessment tool used in vocational counseling. It measures the reinforcing characteristics of a particular job across twenty-one dimensions. There are two forms to the test, one for employees and another for supervisors. Both forms are gender neutral, can be used with groups or individuals, and are appropriate for those reading at a fifth-grade level or higher. Administration time is approximately twenty minutes. Scoring of the test is best done by a computer program.

118. D: A warning sign that a counselor is developing a relationship with a client that is too personal is the counselor's asking the client about personal matters unrelated to the client's needs. It's common to enjoy interacting with some clients more than others or even feel some attraction to a client, but the counselor should recognize signs and avoid acting on any attraction or showing preference for one client over others, maintaining a professional relationship at all times.

119. D: Cognitive development was NOT identified as a major determinant in Ann Roe's theory, which is a needs-based approach. She believed that occupational selection is a function of the needs developed by a child, whose structure were influenced by a combination of genetics, environmental experiences, and interactions between the parents and the child. Career development as a part of cognitive development is more closely identified with Tiedeman, O'Hara, and Miller-Tiedeman's decision-making model of career development.

120. B: A narcissistic client is only interested in issues related to self. His body, thoughts, needs, and anything that is related to him is what seems real. Everything else, as not related to the self, is not perceived as real or of interest by the narcissistic personality. This issue was discussed early in psychology theory. Freud talked about "primary narcissism" as a time when, as infants, individuals are unable to differentiate between self and others. Self-interest is not without its positive aspects, however, as it can be useful in the interest of self-preservation. However, a pathological narcissism

Copyright © Mometrix Media. You have been licensed one copy of this document for personal use only. Any other reproduction or redistribution is strictly prohibited. All rights reserved.

can interfere with interpersonal relationships and social connectedness, leading to further problems in the client's life.

121. A: "The law doesn't allow me to give out any information about clients in order to protect their privacy and safety" is accurate and appropriate. The Health Insurance Portability and Accountability Act (HIPAA) addresses the privacy of health information. It is essential to never release any information or documentation about a client's condition or treatment without consent. Personal information about the client is considered protected health information (PHI), and it includes any identifying or personal information about the client, such as health history, condition, or treatments in any form, and any documentation. Failure to comply with HIPAA regulations can make one liable for legal action.

122. D: ALL of these are circumstances in which testing may be useful to better inform such activities as job or educational placement, counseling, or diagnosis.

123. B: A heterogeneous group is usually more diverse than a homogeneous group. There may be a mixture of ages and genders. Another characteristic of heterogeneous groups is that there are a wide variety of problems as the focus of the group sessions. Homogeneous groups, on the other hand, are generally specific to gender and problem. The participants usually have common characteristics, which leads to strong bonds being formed among group members. Usually there is less conflict and greater attendance in homogeneous groups.

124. B: There are many advantages of group counseling, from cost-effectiveness to the ability to practice skills in a structured setting. There is a great deal of social support as well. Although members have their own individual needs and goals, the purpose of group counseling is for members to become better at interpersonal skills. Group counseling provides feedback and practice for all group members.

125. A: Both Freud's and Ellis' counseling styles would favor an etic approach as both types of counseling use the same techniques for everybody regardless of the individual client's personality or problems. An emic approach, which emphasizes individual differences rather than similarities. Thus, it would be favored by practitioners of Carl Rogers' person-centered counseling or Adler's individual psychology.

126. C: Four key elements identified in building a helping relationship are: 1) Human relations core – empathy, respect, genuineness; 2) Social influence core – competence, power, intimacy; and (as identified by Stanley Strong in his social influence model), expertness, attractiveness, and trustworthiness; 3) Skills core – micro-skills (as identified by Allen Ivey): communication skills such as attending, inquiry, and reflection; and, 4) Theory core – theoretical knowledge that helps therapists to understand the self, interpersonal relationships, interpersonal skills, clients' problems, and to choose effective interventions. Answer B identifies empathy, which is included as part of the human relations core, but none of the other elements is correct. Answer D includes the core concepts of social influence and theory, but none of the other elements. Answer A contains all incorrect elements.

127. A: A displaced homemaker may have worked outside of the home prior to starting a family, but struggles to reenter the workforce afterwards. A re-entry woman is one who had worked, decided to be a stay-at-home mother until her children were old enough to be in school all day, and then returned to work in her chosen profession. Gender bias relates to experiencing discrimination for being in a job that is dominated by the opposite sex. Wage discrimination relates to earning less than someone else while doing the same job.

Copyright © Mometrix Media. You have been licensed one copy of this document for personal use only. Any other reproduction or redistribution is strictly prohibited. All rights reserved.

128. B: Jungian therapists believe in a collective unconscious. Another key concept of Jungian therapy is the archetype. The goal of Jungian therapy is to transform the self by gaining knowledge about the self (collective unconscious, archetypes, personal unconscious) and then recognizing and integrating all aspects of the self (archetypes, etc.).

129. D: There are several criticisms of Rogerian therapy. One common criticism is that while Carl Rogers does take the unconscious into account in his writings, he doesn't give it enough emphasis. Likewise, Rogers doesn't incorporate information relative to developmental stages into his therapy. Rogers is also sometimes criticized because his therapeutic method is not appropriate for use with some types of mental illness. For example, some individuals may not have the ability for self-expression, or feel anxiety for their actions. Rogers' theory also assumes that people are basically good and healthy, so application with clients who are particularly violent or lacking in personal or social conscience may be difficult.

130. C: Berne, who created transactional analysis (a cognitive model of therapy), believed that the personality has three ego states – parent, adult, and child. He felt that people will play various games, which he named in his book Games People Play, to avoid intimacy. The book I'm OK – You're OK was written by Thomas Harris. Harris extended Berne's transactional analysis by positing four basic life positions: "I'm OK – You're OK;" "I'm OK – You're Not OK;" "I'm Not OK – You're Not OK;" and "I'm Not OK – You're OK." The book In And Out of the Garbage Can was authored by Fritz Perls, the founder of Gestalt therapy. The book On Becoming a Person was written by Carl Rogers, whose therapy focused on the "process of becoming," which moves clients toward self-actualization.

131. B: One of the fastest-growing trends in family structures is the multigenerational family, in which the grandparents are raising their grandchildren. They, instead of the children's biological parents, are parenting the grandchildren. Blended families have been around for decades, as have single-parent families. The homosexual family is an acknowledged family structure but is not one of the fastest-growing trends in family structures.

132. A: Rational-Emotive Behavior Therapy (REBT), by Albert Ellis, deals not only with behaviors and feelings, but also with the thoughts behind them. Irrational ideas are believed to be the basic reason for the unpleasant and/or unwanted feelings and behaviors of a client. Ellis theorized that there are twelve core irrational beliefs that can cause or sustain psychological difficulties. One of those core beliefs is that the significant others of an individual must love them for nearly anything they do, instead of the healthier focus on self-respect and loving others without expectation of love being returned.

133. A: The psychodynamic model is monadic as it focuses on the individual's intrapsychic conflicts and their impact on familial relations. The experiential model is dyadic as it focuses on dysfunctional interactions between two family members such as marital partners or siblings. The transgenerational model is triadic as it focuses on conflicts in the interactions between more than two family members. The strategic model is both dyadic and triadic as it will focus on problems occurring both between two family members as well as among three members of reciprocal relationships in a family.

134. C: J. P. Guilford was an American psychologist known primarily for his study of intellectual ability and individual differences. He also did research in creativity, which he associated with "divergent thinking." He believed that intelligence testing wouldn't be as effective with divergent thinking/creative people so he developed special tests for divergent thinkers, which are used with gifted children and others. He believed that creative people could actually achieve lower IQ scores because of the manner in which they approached the testing. He was one of the early theorists who

Copyright © Mometrix Media. You have been licensed one copy of this document for personal use only. Any other reproduction or redistribution is strictly prohibited. All rights reserved.

believed intelligence to be a complex, diverse issue, and that a variety of differences and abilities must be taken into account.

135. B: Antipsychotic (or neuroleptic) medications have been in use since the 1950s and are quite effective overall for schizophrenia. These medications work by affecting neurotransmitters in the brain. They are not, however, a cure-all. The need for medication is highly individualized and may or may not work depending upon the situation. Some patients are helped a great deal, but for others the medications aren't effective. Antipsychotic drugs are often particularly helpful with delusions and hallucinations. Reported side effects include weight gain, drowsiness, muscle spasms, fidgeting, shaking, or stiffness, and sometimes heart problems. Commonly prescribed antipsychotic medications are quetiapine, chlorpromazine, and aripiprazole.

136. B: If using functional family therapy (FFT) to work with the family of a 17-year-old client with antisocial behavior and a history of escalating delinquency, the first phase is **engagement/motivation**, during which the counselor helps the family identify maladaptive beliefs in order to increase expectations for change, reduce negativity and blaming, and increase respect for differences. The second phase is **behavior change** in which the parents used behavioral interventions to improve family function, and the third phase is **generalization** of the skills learned to other environments.

137. B: Krumboltz is a behaviorist and, therefore, is interested not only in genetic endowment but in environmental factors and learning experiences. Holland developed the SDS, which involves looking at an individual's personality characteristics and matching them to clusters of job skills or interests. Therefore, Holland believes that career choices are expressions of one's personality. Roe's theory is developmental and includes not only aspects of one's personality, but genetics, parent–child relationships, and one's early experiences.

138. A: Object relations theory, which is based on Freudian psychoanalytic concepts, gives this chronology of stages: 1) Fusion with mother – sometimes called "normal infantile autism," and occurs in the first 3-4 weeks of life. 2) Symbiosis with mother – which takes place during the 3rd to 8th month of life. 3) Separation/individuation – which starts in the 4th or 5th month of life. 4) Constancy of self and object – which is achieved by the 36th month of life. This theory states that progressing through these consecutive stages gives a child a secure basis for later development by engendering trust in the infant that its needs will be met.

139. D: Bipolar disorder is primarily a mood disorder, while schizophrenia is characterized more by disordered thought patterns.

140. B: If a client with antisocial personality disorder asks the counselor a personal question, such as "Do you live with your boyfriend?" the most appropriate response is "It is not appropriate to ask me personal questions." Consequences for inappropriate behavior should be clearly outlined, so the counselor may follow this statement with another: "If you continue to ask inappropriate questions, I will stop our discussion because that is the consequence for this behavior." The counselor should use care not to try to coax or threaten the client into behaving more appropriately.

141. D: The differences we are looking at here are the differences in the formats of tests. The MMPI-A (Minnesota Multiphasic Personality Inventory–Adolescent) and CPI (California Personality Inventory) are based on a true/false format with a fixed choice. They are paper and pencil objective tests. The Rorschach and TAT (Thematic Apperception Test) are projective tests that are subjective in nature. The answers to the stimuli are unlimited. There are no fixed choices. The test taker makes up answers based on the stimulus being presented.

Copyright © Mometrix Media. You have been licensed one copy of this document for personal use only. Any other reproduction or redistribution is strictly prohibited. All rights reserved.

142. D: Erich Fromm believed that family, politics, or any other form of authoritative power can destroy an individual's potential. He had similar concerns about religion. Erich Fromm felt that religious faith and experience was fine. He didn't take a stand against religious belief in and of itself, but rather had concerns about some aspects of it, and its possible negative effects. He believed that religious tenets could be used to encourage divisiveness and warfare, and that some principles were misdated and misguided (which could possibly lead to harmful choices). He didn't like the authoritarian value system, and focused on the need for individuals to use reason and independent thought in making decisions.

143. A: If a counselor is focusing on social skills training with a client with schizophrenia in order to improve the client's ability to function socially and is using shaping to reinforce teaching, the best description of shaping is rewarding improvement steps toward the target behavior goal. Thus, shaping is a form of positive reinforcement and helps to reinforce the client's sense of self-esteem and achievement. Most clients with schizophrenia have difficulty interacting socially with others and may, for example, exhibit inappropriate facial expression, tone of voice, and interactions.

144. A: Confidentiality has limits. The professional counselor is ethically bound to report certain things. The patient's intent to hurt someone else, suicidal ideation, and the abuse or neglect of a child are all examples of times when the professional counselor may break confidentiality and report what the patient has disclosed. The first session with a patient should also include a discussion of privacy and specific review of the types of information that would need to be reported, and to whom, given particular situations.

145. A: A "token economy" is a behavior modification technique. Tokens (a tangible, material item) are given to the client when target behaviors occur. The client can later turn his tokens in for something of a more significant value. This modification method is useful in settings such as mental hospitals and school classrooms. It has been sometimes criticized for creating a system in which the clients are too attached to the token system, and once the system is ended, the positive effects also cease to exist. This operant conditioning approach has the ultimate goal of seeing the positive behavior continue even after the token system is eventually eliminated.

146. A: "Scaffolding" is a term used by Vygotsky that explains what Susie's mother is doing. She is adjusting her level of support to Susie based on Susie's level of performance. The zone of proximal development involves a range of tasks that are too difficult for the child to do alone but possible to do with the help of adults or other, more-skilled children. "Assisted discovery" is another term used by Vygotsky to describe learning situations that a teacher sets up within a classroom so that children are guided into discovering learning. Learning by imitation is a type of learning that involves a child watching someone perform a task and later performing the task by herself.

147. D: When court-ordered to reveal confidential information about a client, the counselor must of course ethically consider, first and foremost, the counseling relationship, and the rights of the client. He should, if at all possible, obtain written permission from the client to divulge personal information. Failing that, the counselor must use his best professional judgment to limit the amount of information shared with the court. An emphasis must be placed upon sharing information in a way that would be as respectful as possible toward the confidentiality of the client and cause the least possible damage to the counseling relationship.

148. D: If a 27-year-old client with narcissistic personality disorder is pregnant and has made plans to have an abortion but the counselor is opposed to abortion for religious reasons, the counselor should support the client's decision. The client has the legal right to make this decision, and the

Copyright © Mometrix Media. You have been licensed one copy of this document for personal use only. Any other reproduction or redistribution is strictly prohibited. All rights reserved.

counselor must use care not to impose personal religious beliefs onto the client or try to pressure the client into making a different decision.

149. C: Internal validity asks, "Did the treatment clearly cause the effect?" External validity asks the question, "Can you generalize the results?" Thus, the selection of subjects can affect both. Internal validity is compromised if comparison groups have different compositions (e.g., if they were not randomly selected), making it unclear if the outcome resulted simply from different kinds of persons in each group. Selection of subjects can also affect external validity if the subjects were not randomly selected, as the results may only apply to other similar individuals, such as college students, and cannot be generalized to the larger population. Attrition would affect internal validity if subjects drop out of the study since results could be very different without the continued presence of those subjects. External validity would not be as directly affected by attrition as internal validity. Instrumentation would affect internal validity if the measurement instruments are inaccurate or are changed during the study, or if there are human recording errors. In these cases, instrumentation would be a confounding variable and it would more pertinent to internal than external validity. Experimenter bias could influence subjects' responses, which would confound internal validity. External validity would be more confounded by subject reactions or lack of ecological validity if the setting or circumstances of the study are so unusual that generalization is impossible.

150. A: Since the evidence-based SAFE-T tool indicates that the client is at low risk for suicide because risks (such as access to guns and health concerns) are modifiable and protective factors (such as religious beliefs and social supports) are strong, the intervention that is most indicated is outpatient treatment with crisis numbers to call if the client needs support. The SAFE-T tool has 5 steps: (1) assessment of risk factors, (2) assessment of protective factors, (3) suicide inquiry (specific questions about plans, intent, ideation), (4) assignment of risk level (low, moderate, high) and appropriate intervention, and (5) documentation and plans.

151. A: The more closely related two things are, the greater the number of predictions that can be made about each from the other. A correlation strategy seeks to determine how strong the relation is between things. For example, one might wish to conduct an experiment related to health issues, and therefore propose that high levels of stress and high blood pressure go together. Although that statement alone doesn't mean that one causes the other, it does provide valuable information and further the scientific study of that issue.

152. B: "V" codes are used when what is being treated is not classified as a mental disorder but is the focus of treatment. An example of this would be uncomplicated bereavement. In the DSM coding system, the V replaces the first digit of the five-digit code.

153. A: The OOH is the Occupational Outlook Handbook. This handbook provides information about trends in occupations, as well as statistics about salaries and wages. The DOT is not the Department of Transportation; it is the Dictionary of Occupational Titles and is obsolete. It has been replaced by the Occupational Information Network (O*NET). Basically, the DOT listed nine occupational categories such as professional, technical, managerial, clerical, and sales careers. The Wall Street Journal is a reliable source for information about the financial and business world but is not a source for looking at trends in occupations. The SOC is the Standard Occupational Classification Manual, which classifies types of activities associated with different careers. It does not provide information about trends in occupations.

154. A: Significance level means the degree to which one is likely to make a mistake in either rejecting or accepting the null hypothesis when they should not (i.e., There is not a significant

Copyright © Mometrix Media. You have been licensed one copy of this document for personal use only. Any other reproduction or redistribution is strictly prohibited. All rights reserved.

difference between experimental groups but the null hypothesis is rejected, or there is indeed a significant difference but the null hypothesis that there is not is accepted). Conventions of experimental research tend to use significance levels of .05, .01, or .001. A level of .01, as in this question, means that one is willing to accept the possibility of error in one out of one hundred experimental trials. Significance level does not refer to actually executing the experiment itself wrongly, nor does it refer to errors of instrumentation or to the hypothesis itself being incorrect. Additionally, in answer D, "ten out of one hundred" is wrong. In answer C, "one out of ten" is also wrong.

155. D: Post-traumatic stress disorder (PTSD) is an anxiety disorder that involves the client experiencing anxiety-related symptoms long after the original stressful event took place. Those in the military, crime victims, and survivors of natural disasters are common populations affected by this disorder, as are children who suffer trauma. Flashbacks, nightmares, physical symptoms (e.g., intestinal issues, weight gain), and memory and sleep difficulties are just a few of the possible symptoms associated with PTSD. Following evaluation and diagnosis, treatment for PTSD is often psychotherapy and medication. Behavioral techniques, such as desensitization, are also sometimes used effectively.

156. C: Larry is in Stage 5 (the first of Kohlberg's two postconventional stages) where social contracts exist and most rules are relative; Carol is in stage 6, the second of the postconventional level: universal ethical principles apply in a self-chosen orientation, and the individual may or may not obey a law depending on whether they believes it is the right or moral thing to do. Kohlberg's first preconventional level consists of stage 1 which has a punishment and obedience orientation (i.e., we must obey the law or be punished); and stage 2, which has a hedonistic and instrumental orientation (i.e., we must obey the law to get rewarded). Kohlberg's second conventional level consists of stage 3, where an interpersonal acceptance orientation is predominant (i.e., we must follow the rules to get approval); and stage 4, where a law and order orientation prevails (e.g., we must obey the laws to conform to authority). The postconventional and highest level with Stages 5 and 6 is the level and stages of Larry's and Carol's respective moral development.

157. B: Glasser is associated with reality therapy, while the other three are Neo-Freudians. Karen Horney is associated with object relations, Jung with the collective unconscious and archetypes, and Adler with birth order and family constellations.

158. A: An effective method to evaluate the progress of a group therapy session is to have an outside observer sit in on a session or two, and evaluate the group dynamics. Using the group facilitator or counselor to evaluate the group may not always be the most effective method, as the counselor would be evaluating his/her own performance. Likewise, group members are ineffective at evaluating the group because of their personal involvement and possible lack of objectivity. An outside observer brings an objective view to the situation and can more easily point out possible difficulties between group members, and between the group and the facilitator.

159. C: Children who are diagnosed with conduct disorder at a young age (preteen) are most at risk of developing antisocial personality disorder as adults. Those who develop conduct disorder during adolescence are more amenable to treatment. Adults with antisocial personality disorder have a persistent lack of regard for others and violate the rights of others beginning during childhood or early adolescence although the diagnosis is only made after the person turns 18 and has exhibited symptoms since age 15.

160. C: Feminist therapists believe that the personal is political, and that personal and societal identities are interdependent. They believe that intrapsychic, interpersonal, and contextual

Copyright © Mometrix Media. You have been licensed one copy of this document for personal use only. Any other reproduction or redistribution is strictly prohibited. All rights reserved.

variables help in defining distress. Therefore, they use an integrated analysis of oppression including society's gender expectations and oppression based on race, ethnicity, culture, and sexual orientation. They believe that the counseling relationship is egalitarian and that women's perspectives are valued. They reject androcentric norms and accept subjective experience and feminist consciousness. The qualities listed in the question, when taken as a whole, do not uniquely relate to SFBT, narrative therapy, or reality therapy.

161. C: Labeling is NOT a reason testing should be used. Even though some tests will yield scores which can assign a person to a level of giftedness or intellectual disability, using this categorization via scores for labeling a person should be avoided as it is stigmatizing and can limit the individual's educational, vocational, life options and ultimate success. Testing is useful for understanding oneself better, for obtaining licensure or certification via passing test scores, and for appropriately planning a person's educational programs.

162. B: Francis Galton was a British psychologist. Charles Darwin was his cousin, and perhaps encouraged by his cousin's writings, Galton developed a keen interest in heredity. Just as in Darwin's work with the plant and animal world, Galton hypothesized that individual personality traits (and particularly intellectual superiority), were inherited. In 1869, Galton's book *Hereditary Genius* outlined his belief that superior abilities and intellect were handed down generation to generation. He is often called "the father of behavioral genetics" for his work with twins, and also founded the first mental testing center.

163. C: Albert Bandura believed that behavior and reinforcement did not always have to take place for learning to occur. He believed that "modeling" (or learning just by seeing someone else do something) was a significant type of learning. If one could only learn by trial and error, the cost of errors could be too costly and so modeling is a far more reasonable way to learn. Bandura also theorized that observational learning happens through cognition. Imagining oneself in the same situation as someone else causes the modeling to successfully occur. Because of its cognitive nature, there's a lot of opportunity for creativity with modeling as well. As the individual imagines himself in the same situation; he may combine more than one situation to attain learning of it, thus producing a more creative process.

164. C: Adler did not examine irrational beliefs in his family therapy. He was concerned with feelings of inferiority, social interest, and goals of behavior. Just as with individual therapy, rational-emotive family therapy looks at irrational beliefs.

165. B: By definition, reliability refers to how consistent over time a test is. Validity is defined as having a test measure what it is supposed to measure. Standardization refers to a set of procedures that are consistently followed for each administration of a test. Although it describes consistency, it is not related to the test itself. Standardization refers to the procedures implemented while giving a test.

166. D: If a client with borderline personality disorder vacillates between insisting that her father is a kind and loving father and a horrible abusive monster, this is an example of splitting, which is a type of defense mechanisms common to people with this disorder. The client keeps opposing feelings separate and fails to integrate them so that the client's emotional responses may swing quickly back and forth from one extreme to another.

Copyright © Mometrix Media. You have been licensed one copy of this document for personal use only. Any other reproduction or redistribution is strictly prohibited. All rights reserved.

167. D: 5 years. Stages of recovery from addiction:

1. **Initiation:** Client enters a program or tries to control addiction without help.
2. **Early abstinence** (first 90 days): Client may undergo withdrawal and is at risk for relapse. Needs to learn coping skills and tools to help avoid further addiction.
3. **Maintenance** (after 90 days and up to 5 years): Client should focus on avoiding relapse and learning about triggers. improving relationships with others and anger management.
4. **Advanced recovery:** The client has remained free of addiction for 5 years but must remain vigilant, may need to attend 12-step meetings or ongoing support groups or counseling.

168. A: In William Glasser's choice theory (renamed from "control theory"), there are five fundamental psychological needs. "Survival" is the first, which is paid little attention to unless threatened. "Love and Belonging" is next, indicating that we, as humans, all have a basic need for acceptance. The third stage is for "Power/Recognition," referring to the individual goals that people have, and the need to achieve those goals on some level. "Freedom" comes fourth, and ties into our sense of fair play and need to have a choice in our lives. Finally, the last fundamental psychological need is for "fun," which is the ultimate goal for pleasure.

169. B: If the counselor finds a client with PTSD and flashbacks cowering in the corner of the room in a state of panic, the best approach is to say, "I know you are afraid, but you are safe here." The counselor should acknowledge the client's fears while trying to use grounding techniques to remind the client that he is safe. The counselor should not attempt to reach out to the client or touch the client without first asking for permission as this may trigger a violent response.

170. C: From a multicultural perspective, an emic view considers that an individual's culture matters. On the other hand, an etic view considers that people are people no matter where they come from or what their cultural background is. Another way to think about this distinction is as emic = culture matters, and etic = total world. The distinction between autoplastic and alloplastic is that the former believes in the efficacy of changes taking place within the individual, while the latter believes in making changes in the environment.

171. B: A major criticism of Levinson's work is that he only studied men. In fact, his most famous book is entitled The Seasons of a Man's Life. Critics argue that this limits his findings, since they cannot be applied to women. It is erroneous to say that his developmental periods did not include transitions. He actually named three major transitions between his four major eras of a man's life: the early adult transition, the mid-life transition, and the late adult transition. It is likewise false that many critics have argued against the existence of a midlife crisis. While there may be a few who would take this position, a far greater number agree that midlife is often a time of questioning and/or reevaluating one's life. It is also not true that Levinson's midlife crisis excluded questioning one's career. He actually made the point that career is one part of life that men tend to question in their 40s, and that this is a common time for some men to change their occupations.

172. A: The key word here is "distort." The most reasonable answer is that stereotypes distort (exaggerate) one's ideas about how one group is different from another group. In reality, the differences between groups are not as extreme as stereotypes make them out to be. People of differing cultures are not so different from people from another culture.

173. D: The Johari window got its name from the two individuals who developed the concept—Joe Luft and Harry Ingham. They believed that clients come into counseling with all sorts of information, some of it known to the client and others, some unknown to the client but known by others, some known only by the client, and some unknown by everyone. Luft and Ingham believed

Copyright © Mometrix Media. You have been licensed one copy of this document for personal use only. Any other reproduction or redistribution is strictly prohibited. All rights reserved.

that it is important to uncover that which is unknown. The collective unconscious is associated with Carl Jung. Neurolinguistic programming, or NLP, is a system of treatment that integrates psychology, linguistics, and communications. It was created by Richard Bandler and John Grinder. The family constellation is part of Adlerian counseling.

174. B: Using testing to critique the client's performance in school, work, or training is a LESS appropriate rationale for a counselor to use testing. The client's teacher, employer, or trainer would be a more appropriate person to critique performance, and they will sometimes use tests to aid in their evaluations. When a counselor uses tests, it can often help to predict the client's future performance in educational, training, or workplace settings. Testing can also help clients to make decisions about their educational or occupational futures. A counselor can also administer and interpret certain tests to help clients discover other interests they have of which they may have been unaware. This can help give clients insight into things they might like to do which they had never previously considered.

175. D: Integrative counseling synthesizes existing theories and practices from a variety of theoretical perspectives (as opposed to just borrowing them). Thus, it implies that a model is being created. Integrative counseling is not the same as eclectic counseling which also uses a variety of techniques and theories. Integrative counseling goes beyond this to form a unique, synthesized theory. Integrative counseling begins with the counselor developing a personal theory rather than ending with it. The counselor's process of theory development results in a highly individualistic theory instead of a highly generalized one. Therefore, it is highly congruent and does not make much use of incongruity. The theory is also highly flexible.

176. B: Harrington and Glasser were proponents of reality therapy where the process of transference (i.e., when a client unconsciously expresses feelings toward the therapist which are really feelings toward a past significant other) is rejected. Reality therapists are solution-oriented and focus on the present. They feel transference is unnecessary if the therapist is authentic (i.e., being himself or herself in therapy). Answers A and D are positions typical of Freudian psychoanalysis, wherein transference is found beneficial to treatment. They believe it is inevitable in therapy, and encourage it so analysis of transference can be done to gain insights to the client's unconscious. Answer C is a position typical of a behaviorist; unconscious states are disregarded, and only observable behaviors are considered. In learning theories, external behaviors can be changed. According to Skinner, whatever internal feelings motivate the behavior will not matter because they cannot be seen and thus cannot be environmentally manipulated.

177. D: There are several stages common to group therapy dynamics. Forming is the initial stage when group members are first placed together, and members tend to be rather cautious during this stage. The second stage is called Storming, when group members begin to familiarize themselves with each other and test limits. Norming occurs when conflicts begin to be worked out, and some level of cohesiveness is achieved. In the Performing stage, the group is at its most mature and working toward common goals. The final stage is Adjourning, and is just as it sounds, the act of disbanding the group.

178. D: There are a number of ethical violations in this scenario. The most blatant is requiring clients to purchase these materials. The counselor seeks to profit from the purchase of these materials, which is ethically wrong. Another issue related to this scenario is that the requirements for purchase set up a power differential that should be avoided. The counselor might consider this double-dipping where she gets paid by the insurance company to provide treatment and she profits from the sale of her own materials.

Copyright © Mometrix Media. You have been licensed one copy of this document for personal use only. Any other reproduction or redistribution is strictly prohibited. All rights reserved.

179. C: Delusion of reference: Client believes everything in the environment references her, such as the client believing that messages are being sent to her in newspapers, magazines, radio, and television and that she must decipher them. **Delusion of persecution**: Client believes others intend to harm her. **Delusion of control**: Client believes other people or objects control her actions. **Delusion of grandeur**: Client believes she is an important person or being, such as God.

180. B: If a client nearing the end-of-life because of a terminal disease tells the counselor that she feels that her life was wasted, guiding the client to carry out a life review may be beneficial because it can help the client focus not only on the disappointments in her life but also the achievements and things that brought happiness to herself or others. Reviewing memories and feelings and re-examining one's life can help the person to come to terms with the past and find resolution.

181. A: A statistical norm would measure how people actually act, but a cultural norm is all about expectations and how people are supposed to behave in that particular culture. In fact, some professionals suggest that it is simply a group of cultural norms that makes a particular culture. Social norms are expected to be adhered to within a culture, and there is usually a penalty for breaking those norms. A norm may be something like the style of clothing that is appropriate to wear in a given situation (like wearing black to a funeral in the United States), or taking one's place at the end of a customer service line instead of just cutting into the front of the line. Breaking accepted, and expected, cultural norms can result in simple irritation on the part of others or even in being ostracized from the culture.

182. A: When involved in therapy with children, it is often useful to include parents in the sessions. There are several reasons why this can be a positive addition to therapy. Parents provide an added sense of security for the child, especially in cases in which the child is very young. In cases in which the child is shy or fearful, the initial inclusion of a parental figure can be critical to the success of future sessions, as it eases the child into a relationship with the counselor (that can later more effectively become independent of parental involvement). In cases in which a child is resistant to therapy or even aggressive, the presence of a parent can aid the counselor in obtaining a reasonable level of cooperation from the child.

183. A: It is not considered ethical for a counselor to perform forensic evaluations on a past or current client. It is also not considered ethical for the counselor to enter into a counseling situation with someone they have previously performed a forensic evaluation on.

184. A: The initial intervention for an emotional crisis reflecting psychopathology is to stay with the client and reassure her until her panic subsides. People with BPD often feel insecure and inherently worthless. They are often erratic and have difficulty establishing long-term relationships although symptoms tend to lessen with age. The main feature of borderline personality disorder (BPD) is a persistent pattern of instability in interpersonal relationships, self-image, and emotion. Two-thirds of those diagnosed are female. Characteristics include attempts to avoid real or imagined abandonment and impulsivity in at least 2 areas.

185. C: If a client with substance abuse disorder states he has been using "beanies," the counselor should understand that the client is referring to **methamphetamine**, which is also sometimes referred to as "blue devils," "crank," and "crystal" as well as any number of local names. **Marijuana** is commonly called "weed," "Aunt Mary," "Mary Jane," and "pot." **Cocaine** may be called many names, including "coke," "blow,", "snow," and "sugar." **Heroin** may be called "horse," "H," "Aunt Hazel," "smack," and "charley" as well as many less commonly-used names.

Copyright © Mometrix Media. You have been licensed one copy of this document for personal use only. Any other reproduction or redistribution is strictly prohibited. All rights reserved.

186. D: If a client has been diagnosed with narcissistic personality disorder, the therapy approach that is generally recommended is psychotherapy, focusing on personality traits. Change is often difficult, and the client may require therapy for extended periods before making progress, especially if the client is not motivated to make changes. Those with narcissistic personality disorder typically have little empathy for others and have an elevated sense of their own importance and a strong need for approval and admiration.

187. A: The counselor may recommend reality-based activities (playing cards, engaging in occupational therapy) as an intervention for a client who is having hallucinations. Reality-based activities are distracting, and clients often have difficulty focusing on both the hallucination and the activity. Activities that are calming may also help to reduce hallucinations as they often intensify when the client experiences increased anxiety.

188. C: The MMPI-II is a personality test (the Minnesota Multiphasic Personality Inventory, second edition), while all of the others are part of the Wechsler series of intelligence tests. The WISC-V is the Wechsler Intelligence Scale for Children–fifth edition and is for children aged 6 to 16. The WAIS-IV is the Wechsler Adult Intelligence Scale–fourth edition and is for adults. The WPPSI-IV is the Wechsler Preschool and Primary Scales of Intelligence – fourth edition and is for children between the ages of 3 and 7 years, 3 months.

189. D: This is an example of quid pro quo: "If you do something for me, I'll do something for you." The Premack principle deals with two behaviors that the target would perform. Negative reinforcement deals with the removal of unpleasant consequences when a desired behavior occurs.

190. B: Alfred Adler's birth order theory rejects the idea that children born within the same family, and raised within similar circumstances, are unaffected by the order in which they were born. He believed that one could make determinations about the personality of an individual simply by where in the family birth order the child was placed. For example, the firstborn often suffers from feelings of inferiority because of being dethroned from his place of total attentiveness by subsequent children. The firstborn works hard to follow in his parent's footsteps and embraces responsibility.

191. B: If a client states, "I don't understand. My daughter said that she had to leave town," an appropriate clarifying question would be "Are you confused because you don't know why she had to leave town?" Clarifying questions are utilized to ensure that the listener has understood the meaning (as opposed to just the words) of the client's statement. Clarifying questions often contain some paraphrase of what the client has stated and may include such phrases as "Did I understand you to say...?" or "Did you say...?"

192. B: Richard Lazarus theorized that there were two forms of coping. One type, called "problem-focused coping," is utilized by individuals who face their difficulties directly and try to solve them. This is a more direct approach, facing issues head-on. By contrast, "emotion-focused coping" is used by people who are more likely to avoid their problems, pray for help, rationalize, or use other defense mechanisms. Emotion-focused coping can be productive in times when a delay in dealing with stress is the best course of action; however, overall, problem-focused coping is usually the best strategy.

193. D: If, when assessing a 35-year-old Arab American female, the counselor notes that, while discussing her family, the client uses a louder voice than while discussing other issues, this probably means that issues about her family are of special importance because speaking more loudly about important issues is characteristic of Arab Americans. People in this culture often stand

121

Copyright © Mometrix Media. You have been licensed one copy of this document for personal use only. Any other reproduction or redistribution is strictly prohibited. All rights reserved.

close to others but avoid physical and eye contact with those of the opposite gender. However, it's important to remember what holds true in general for a culture may not hold true for an individual in the culture.

194. A: If a 60-year-old client in a stable long-term relationship comes to see the counselor because he has begun to experience erectile dysfunction, the counselor should consider initially referring the client to a urologist because erectile dysfunction in older males is often associated with medical conditions (such as enlarged prostate) and medications (such as beta blockers). If this is the case, then medical treatment of the underlying cause or medications, such as Viagra®, may benefit the client. If there is no physical/medical cause, then issues, such as performance anxiety and stress, should be explored.

195. B: A displaced homemaker is someone who has been out of the workforce for a period of time and is now having difficulty finding suitable employment. The word "homemaker" is used because quite often the displaced homemaker is someone who has left paid employment to run a household or raise children while supported by another relative. Often, displaced homemakers have a variety of marketable skills, but because of the lapse of time since their last paid position, employers are reluctant to hire them. Displaced homemakers may also struggle with feelings of insecurity and inadequacy, which also may make it difficult for them to effectively market themselves. The difference between a displaced homemaker and a "stay at home mother" is that the displaced homemaker left a career to raise the family while a stay at home mother may or may not have ever worked.

196. A: Acculturation takes place when two different cultures mix together and begin to change. Cultural exchange goes in both directions, but there is usually more change in the smaller, less dominant culture. Because of the changes to the less-dominant culture, there is usually also more stress on that cultural group, which may lead to other problematic issues. In regards to mental health issues related to acculturation, studies have shown a variety of levels of impact, depending upon the particular circumstances. Acculturation issues have been discussed as far back as Plato and have been increasingly studied through recent years.

197. A: When Person A wants to eliminate a previously conditioned response in Person B, Person A withholds any reinforcement when the response occurs so that Person B no longer elicits the behavior. This is known as extinction. Discrimination occurs in classical and operant conditioning when a person learns to respond to only specific stimuli, while not responding to other similar stimuli. The person learns to distinguish between similar stimuli. "Punishment" is also a term associated with operant conditioning. It is a behavior modification technique that is used to decrease the probability that a particular behavior will occur again. Punishment can be either the presentation of an aversive stimulus or the taking away of a positive stimulus. Elimination is not a technique utilized in classical and operant conditioning.

198. A: The most appropriate standard of care for a counselor who works with multicultural clients is to treat each client individually, not the same way. Special concern must be taken to ensure that the counselor is cognizant of her/his own biases; that the counselor becomes familiar with other cultures; and that the counselor can adapt her/his strategies and approaches to what is most efficacious for a particular client.

199. C: In this situation it is appropriate to use a sliding fee scale as the client clearly cannot afford the usual fee. If the counselor were to require him to make installment payments, the counselor would be putting undue burden on him and may cause him emotional and financial harm. The

Copyright © Mometrix Media. You have been licensed one copy of this document for personal use only. Any other reproduction or redistribution is strictly prohibited. All rights reserved.

counselor could make a referral to someone else, but the same scenario may present itself there, too. Refusing to see the client unless he can pay the usual fee is a form of abandonment.

200. A: The National Counselor Examination is a four-hour, paper and pencil test, using a multiple-choice format. The test is given twice a year in various locations and used by many states as a way to determine eligibility to be certified as a professional counselor. It's an objective test because the personal thoughts and feelings of the test-takers are not taken into account. The individual taking the test simply chooses from among the four choices offered for each question. The word "objective" refers to the scoring method used with the particular test, and there is only one right answer to each question.

Copyright © Mometrix Media. You have been licensed one copy of this document for personal use only. Any other reproduction or redistribution is strictly prohibited. All rights reserved.

Thank You

We at Mometrix would like to extend our heartfelt thanks to you, our friend and patron, for allowing us to play a part in your journey. It is a privilege to serve people from all walks of life who are unified in their commitment to building the best future they can for themselves.

The preparation you devote to these important testing milestones may be the most valuable educational opportunity you have for making a real difference in your life. We encourage you to put your heart into it—that feeling of succeeding, overcoming, and yes, conquering will be well worth the hours you've invested.

We want to hear your story, your struggles and your successes, and if you see any opportunities for us to improve our materials so we can help others even more effectively in the future, please share that with us as well. **The team at Mometrix would be absolutely thrilled to hear from you!** So please, send us an email (support@mometrix.com) and let's stay in touch.

If you feel as though you need additional help, please check out the other resources we offer:

> ### Study Guide: http://MometrixStudyGuides.com/CPCE
>
> ### Flashcards: http://MometrixFlashcards.com/CPCE

Copyright © Mometrix Media. You have been licensed one copy of this document for personal use only. Any other reproduction or redistribution is strictly prohibited. All rights reserved.